A Tearful Celebration

Thanks for your support

— Jim Means

Ps. 119:50

A Tearful Celebration

JAMES E. MEANS

MULTNOMAH PRESS
PORTLAND, OREGON 97266

Cover design and illustration by Hilber Nelson
Edited by Jane Franks and Liz Heaney

A TEARFUL CELEBRATION
© 1985 by Multnomah Press
Portland, Oregon 97266

Printed in the United States of America

Library of Congress Cataloging in Publication Data

Means, James E.
　A tearful celebration.

　1. Consolation.　　2. Bereavement—Religious aspects—Christianity.　　3. Means, James E.　　4. Means, Norma.
I. Title.
BV4905.2.M32　　1985　　　　　248.8′6　　　　　85-343
ISBN 0-88070-085-8 (pbk.)

85　86　87　88　89　90　91　–　10　9　8　7　6　5　4　3　2　1

To my children
Don, Kathy, and Susan
whose constant love and support
helped to make our trial triumphant.

Contents

Foreword

The closing moments of Norma's memorial service were unforgettable, emotionally supercharged. Ted Travis, who had studied opera in Vienna before entering seminary, stood beside the closed casket in that crowded sanctuary, lifted his golden voice, and sang:

> Go ahead, drive the nails in my hands,
>   Laugh at me where you stand.
> Go ahead and say it isn't me;
>   The day will come when you will see,
> For I'll rise again;
>   Ain't no power on earth can hold me down.
> Yes, I'll rise again, death can't keep in me in the
>   ground.

It was an electrifying witness to a resurrection-faith which had sustained Norma through her long months of wasting illness. And now that same faith would give comfort and hope to her grieving friends and family.

Jim and I talked together many times after his wife's disease had been diagnosed as terminal malignancy. We had developed a sort of "soul brother" relationship reaching back more than twenty-five years to Jim's student days in seminary. I had ministered in churches where he pastored and I had been graciously entertained in the Means's home. I came to greatly admire Norma's sparkling personality and spiritual strength. Now Jim, an unusually sensitive and profoundly reflective brother, shared with me his intense struggles, his soul-shaking perplexities, and his turbulent feelings as his beloved wife inched her agonized way down into the dark valley of death. And once she was gone, Jim sincerely thanked God for her release from suffering and for her entrance into the presence of the Savior; yet he could not deny either his questions or his emotions.

Having shared with Jim his struggle against demonic doubt and despair, I applaud his integrity and courage in sharing his fierce conflict and battle-scarred faith with all who read these autobiographical probings of life's gospel-illuminated mysteries. What my friend and colleague has given us, written with his psychic blood, is no glib anodyne, no shallow apologetic which would falsely claim that Christianity is a guaranteed panacea for our pain and adversity. Rather, he has written a powerful testimony to God's grace and sovereignty. It will enable anguished mourners to cope in the darkness until the day of renewed joy and trial-tempered trust breaks through and stands triumphant.

Jim's declaration is that of John Bunyan's Hopeful, who, when crossing the dreaded river, said to Christian, "Be of good cheer, my brother; I feel the bottom, and it is good." There is no encouragement like that given by one who has touched bottom and found God's grace sufficient for that ultimate testing of faith.

Vernon C. Grounds

Letter to My Children

Dear Don, Kathy, and Susan:

I have written this book primarily to help you in your struggle with some of life's most basic questions. These are the questions which inevitably arise when the soul is severely tested by suffering. Obviously there are no easy solutions, but what I have offered in these pages is the record of my own effort to discover satisfactory, biblical answers.

The experience of life is very good—and very bad. Beauty is side-by-side with ugliness. We are awed by something wonderful, but then a ghastly deformity ruins it all. In the very midst of great delight some monstrous, grotesque circumstance forces us to the brink of despair. Then despite all that is excellent, we feel seized by some mysterious mischief-maker determined to crush us.

This book grows out of our encounter with the repulsive event of cancer. The physicians called it an infiltrating carcinoma, a malignant tumor in the breast. Like an incarnated vulgarity, it intruded into our family, corrupted our sense of well-being, and claimed the life of your mother.

I have felt the tightening grip of depression. I have known deepening anxiety, like a child lost in a darkening forest. I have drunk the bitter cup of grief. I have wrestled with the great questions of pain. During the days of your mother's sickness, I walked the thin edge of mystery and struggled to find meaning in catastrophe. I was forced to face the fact of my own mortality. Life's ultimate realities were tested in the fire of sorrow.

In that fierce struggle against death I searched for the aggressive faith of the great saints. I wanted that steely, quiet confidence of those godly men and women who rose triumphant out of the cruel calamities of life. As much as I needed that rock-ribbed trust in God for myself, I desired even more to bequeath it as a priceless heritage for you children.

I have tried to avoid trivia and triteness which tempt those who write about suffering. I have looked long and steady at the torture of my soul. I tried to participate in the dying of your mother as much as it is possible for one human to participate in another's death. The water of that river which John Bunyan said is "to the stomach cold" and which "has been a terror to many" has been real to me. In the nightmare of pain and loss I have been astonished at the ways of God, but I have found strength for the present and hope for the future.

My hope and my prayer is that you children will find help within these pages in your own search for faith and meaning. In making this personal record available to others in the collapsing circumstances of life, perhaps they too will discover assistance in the intensely personal, lonely journey toward an invincible faith.

Has God Failed Me?

God's comfort is not insulation from difficulty; it is spiritual fortification sufficient to enable me to stand firm, undefeated in the fiery trials of life.

Has God Failed Me?

How long, O LORD, must I call for help, but you do not listen? Or cry out to you, "Violence!" but you do not save?

Habakkuk 1:2

I STRUGGLE BECAUSE MY WIFE HAS BEEN taken from me and my children; I wonder why God has let us down. The prophet Habakkuk expressed my feelings long ago. He observed injustice all around him, pleaded fervently to God for help, but found that God was not very speedy in righting the wrongs in this world. His complaint struck home: "Why do you make me look at injustice? Why do you tolerate wrong?" (Habakkuk 1:3). I saw a terrible wrong that needed to be righted, but God did not respond in the way I wanted.

So she died. God did not preserve her life here for us. Many people prayed for her life to be spared, but God refused to do it. I reminded God how much we needed her, but God didn't agree. It certainly seemed to me that her life was very important and that God wouldn't let her die, but He did. Like Habakkuk, I called for help, but God didn't answer as I believed He would. I cried out, but God didn't rescue. I feel that God has let me down—and at the very time when I needed Him most. Would it have frustrated God's eternal plan to grant me just this one miracle with deliverance from this sickness? How am I to handle these feelings that God has failed me?

My experience is not unusual. I have been in hospital rooms with godly parents and heard their sincere prayers that the life of their child be spared. The child died. Missionaries entrust themselves to God's safe-keeping, but sometimes are murdered. Couples fervently ask God for a happy marriage, but presently they divorce. What happened to their prayers? Where is the Christian who does not have his own private tragedy to tell?

As I groped for meaning and some answers, I began to realize that somehow faith in God must be harmonized with the brutal facts of life in this present world.

My view of God was shaped many years ago when I first began to learn about Him. I grew up thinking that God is too good and too kind to permit pain. I thought that He would always provide for my necessities, protect me from my enemies, strengthen me for my temptations, and heal my diseases. Others might fail me in my time of distress, but not God! Never. God would always be there to deliver.

I have been in many testimony meetings and never heard anybody say that God had let them down. People always said that God had answered prayer, provided for their wants, and given unexpected blessings. I never heard anyone say: "God has failed me. God has let me down. When I needed God most He turned His back on me. God did not meet my expectation." What confusion such words would have brought to the meeting! Nobody wanted to tarnish God's good reputation by saying such terrible things. Everybody thought it was better to pretend satisfaction with God's treatment of them.

I came to believe that God would always be a safety measure to me. God would relieve stress, bring deliverance, assure safety, and provide wants. If I got sick, God would make me well. If I needed help in school, God would give it. If I needed money, God would send it. I came to think that God was the great Superpower in heaven whose only real concern was to keep His children comfortable and happy. Sometimes in my effort to make Christianity appealing I preached that God wants us all to have "the good life"—plenty of everything pleasant and nothing unpleasant. However, I see now that the Bible does not teach that.

Much of what our religion expresses is sentimentally magnificent, but theologically weak. We frequently teach what we *want* to believe rather than face the naked, sometimes brutal truth. The words of a familiar hymn we sing in church read:

All you may need He will provide,
   God will take care of you;
Nothing you ask will be denied,
   God will take care of you.

I have sung that song ever since childhood, but I don't like to sing it any more. To say "nothing you ask will be denied" is to tell a lie.

The truth is that God does not instantly and always meet all wants of Christians. Such thinking about God is incorrect. I must surrender these erroneous notions. God is not a cosmic nursemaid who can be manipulated to keep me comfortable and happy. Like the apostle Paul and innumerable others, I must learn to live with deprivation and necessity.

But I cannot deny the validity of prayer or the reality of God just because God didn't give me the life of my wife. Prayer is not a way to get God to always do what I want. Prayer is confessing my dependency upon God. Prayer is trusting Him to do what is best. It is not a clever gimmick to get God to be my servant, my private genie. I cannot get God to conform His plan to my will—despite my fervency, my promises of future service, or my goodness. God will not be clubbed into subordination to my wishes.

Prayer does not invariably give me access to a grab bag of goodies. Nobody can honestly say that God has always done exactly what was desired and expected of Him. I have passed through the extraordinary ugliness of Norma's cancerous death. Nobody can say to me "nothing you ask will be denied." I know better. I have given up the clever little clichés I had been taught. I must accept the facts of life which include harsh realities. No longer can I think of God as a celestial insurance policy against pain. God will not live up to that reputation.

In searching the Scripture I began to see that the early believers were honest enough to admit their disappointment with God. Job protested loudly against God's apparent unfairness to him. Moses bitterly complained of God's treatment of him. David repeatedly lamented God's slowness to come to his assistance. Elijah, at the lowest point in his life's journey, prayed to die, he felt so alone and friendless. Jonah did not approve of God's ways. Jeremiah cried, "Why is my pain unending and my wound grievous and incurable? Will you [God] be to me like a deceptive brook, like a spring that fails?" (Jeremiah 15:18). Habakkuk felt God did not care about his grievance and did not answer his prayers. Paul experienced great distress, anguish of heart, and burning necessity. Has there ever been a true saint who has not struggled with the feeling that God was not treating him fairly? Surely such inner wrestling is one of life's most inescapable trials.

Nowhere in the Bible could I find an absolute guarantee of pleasant circumstances. Christians, like others, are subject to sickness, accident, and incalculable loss. If I think God will always keep me comfortable, I am going to feel let down. God will not always do it. Christians are not exempt from trouble.

The true Christian teaching is: "Our present sufferings are not worth comparing with the glory that will be revealed in us" (Romans 8:18). Peter wrote: "Do not be surprised at the painful trial you are suffering, as though something strange were happening to you" (1 Peter 4:12). I must refuse to be deluded into thinking that life here and now is the wonderful life. The wonderful life is the one to come after this one is over. Here and now there is inevitable groaning as I meet these hard experiences of life, so that "we ourselves, who have the firstfruits of the Spirit, groan inwardly as we wait eagerly for our adoption as sons, the redemption of our bodies" (Romans 8:23). I hurt, I sorrow, I agonize over the loss that has come into my life. A precious life has been taken away. I feel great grief and pain. It sears my every waking hour.

At a time like this, it is imperative that I remember that God has not promised to keep my life bubbling with good, pleasing sensations. I must not prostitute God by giving Him the responsibility of being an indulgent Santa Claus in the heavens. God is not my servant. I am *His* servant.

As I come to grips with my grief, I reject the obnoxious form of sentimentalized, sickly religion so popular today. God's comfort is not insulation from difficulty; it is spiritual fortification sufficient to enable me to stand firm, undefeated in the fiery trials of life. God's provision is not always the green pastures and still waters. Sometimes God leads into the valley of the shadow, but I may walk there with confidence.

No longer can I offer a mindless, frivolous assertion that God always measures up to my every expectation of Him and always gives His children goodies. I must declare that there is that which is beyond my human understanding in the ways of God. Those mysteries have destroyed my comfortable existence, but I proclaim: "Though he slay me, yet will I hope in him" (Job 13:15). I will hurt for years to come. A hundred times a day I feel keenly the void left by death's cruel blow. That pain, however, must drive me to stronger trust in God whose providence is not always compatible with my wishes.

I have made a startling discovery: God does fail at times. He fails to keep His children comfortable. He fails to do everything we think He should do. He fails to dispose His power to our capricious whims. He fails to change His sovereign purposes to please our desires. These failings, however, do not alter my devotion to a God whose wisdom is superior to mine. Eventually I will see that God's eternal purposes are incomparably good for me.

As I grappled with this truth I also saw that in the more important things, God does not fail. The provision of God is adequate for my pilgrimage. God does not fail to see, know, understand, care, love, and ultimately to work all things "in conformity with the purpose of his will" (Ephesians 1:11). His love is constant, though sometimes unfelt. His presence is assured, though sometimes He seems far away. His plan is good, though sometimes I hurt. For this present time I see dimly mere faint outlines of all God's purposes and plans. Yet I believe that His ways are better and His thoughts are higher than my own. My understanding is not crucial. It is my *faith* that is the great, indispensable necessity.

God did not coddle the biblical saints with an unbroken stream of blessing. Their lives, like ours today, were lived in the shadows and valleys of life's tough journey of faith. They got sick. Their children broke their hearts. They failed. They faced trouble of all kinds. They hurt and cried. They complained bitterly. However, in spite of pain and disappointment, sin and failure, they were people of faith. They trusted God despite harsh circumstances. They were steadfast in the face of crushing reality. They hoped in God when all reason for hope was taken away. Such tireless faith is to be our chief goal in life, for by it we glorify God and purchase a place of honor in His kingdom.

We must cultivate this faith. Oftentimes God does not give us what we want, but He gives us strength to pass triumphantly through the difficult times. We do not always understand what has happened, but we choose to trust God anyway.

God has failed to do what I thought He should do, but I must not allow this event to result in any bitterness in me. Instead, I must recognize that this major disappointment should drive me to stronger trust in God. Life looks very different without the false security of an indulgent, over-protective God, but it is more real, honest, and challenging to my faith. It offers greater opportunity to bear witness to a God of wisdom and superior grace.

Shall I Blame God?

They fail to understand that the goodness of God is an ultimate goodness, not a goodness that always pleases the senses of finite man.

Shall I Blame God?

He throws me into the mud, and
I am reduced to dust and ashes.

Job 30:19

I HAVE COME FACE TO FACE WITH ONE OF the most bitter experiences in life—death. I grieve. I feel that life has caved in and I am in some black mudhole. I feel like the psalmist who cried: "You [God] have put me in the lowest pit, in the darkest depths" (Psalm 88:6). Were the biblical writers correct in holding God responsible for their trouble? Is God to blame for the death of my wife? I wrestle with these questions.

I know God created a world in which there are awful possibilities. He allowed His perfect creation to rebel against Him. That brought forth an imperfect world, a world full of sin, sickness, death, and grief. Therefore man must live with trouble and inevitable agony.

It was a great shock when I discovered for the first time that terrible tragedy does happen. When I was a young ministerial student, Norma and I went on a short vacation in western Colorado. On a beautiful Saturday morning, Labor Day weekend, we entered the inspiring Glenwood Canyon which contains the Colorado River. Rounding a bend in the highway, we noticed a small group of people looking down over the bank into the water. There in the river, upside down, was a car with only the four wheels showing above the swift current. Standing on the car was a young man, hardly more than a boy, anguished beyond description. He looked up at us, utterly overwhelmed, and with outstretched arms, screamed repeatedly: *"My God, somebody do something! My wife's in there!"*

His bride of two days had been driving the car laden with wedding gifts, some still unopened. He was following her in a pickup truck as they moved to their first apartment. The new husband watched with horror as his wife attempted to pass, lost control, and plunged into the river. Life, which moments before had seemed so bright and promising, had suddenly collapsed. A lumber truck, with a cable and winch, pulled the car from the cold waters. The body of his beautiful bride was lifted from the front seat as the water ran off the wedding gifts.

Such unspeakable tragedy is common. It is an inevitable part of living in this imperfect, sin-cursed world. Suddenly (it always seems sudden) the tidal wave of trouble washes over the soul. Then there are feelings of helplessness, loneliness, despair, anger, and sorrow. The time of affliction comes to all. The bubble of prosperity eventually bursts.

Tragedies come in various forms. People die. Some fail in a crucial moment of testing. Children rebel. Financial security collapses. Health fails. Accidents cripple. Marriages sever. Disasters are endless. Their consequence is grief, emotional trauma, different for each individual, yet somehow the same for all. We often blame God for our tragedies.

How grateful I have been for the authenticity of the writers of Scripture! They made no effort to cover up their depressions. They were honest about their feelings. They were not afraid to admit that they had hit bottom. They frequently felt no comfort, even in God. They sometimes held God responsible for their grief.

Job felt abandoned by God in his misery. He lost his security, his children, and his health. He sat in the dust and ashes, scraping himself with broken pieces of pottery, mourning his pathetic condition. He was unable to discern God's presence, concern, or purpose. He felt God had cast him into his disastrous situation.

Even Jesus Christ became deeply distressed, truly amazed at the awful depths of Gethsemane. He was stunned with the enormity of His agony, crying: "My soul is overwhelmed with sorrow to the point of death" (Matthew 26:38). He felt no comfort and no presence of the Father. Countless believers have cried out: "My God, my God, why have you forsaken me?" (Psalm 22:1) and "O my God, I cry out by day, but you do not answer" (Psalm 22:2). In the hours of tragedy we often feel God has abandoned us. We blame Him and we think He does not care that we are hurting.

In this time of distress I have no easy answers to the questions which torture my mind. No question, however, carries such mental and spiritual turmoil as the question: "Is this monstrous event God's retribution for my sin?" Did God inflict cancer because of my personal stupidity, negligence, or disobedience? Would my wife be alive today if I had appreciated her a little more? Did God let her die because He was displeased with me? Such thinking, straight from Job's friends, suggests that suffering is always evidence of the disfavor of God. This teaching must be rejected. God's loving discipline must not be equated with life's atrocities such as cancer.

Job did not suffer because of his sin. Lazarus did not die because he had done wrong, but "for God's glory so that God's Son may be glorified through it" (John 11:4). Similarly, a man was born blind not because of his sin or the sin of his parents, but "so that the work of God might be displayed in his life" (John 9:3).

How can we trust or love God if we think He would inflict such punishment upon us? How can we worship God if we believe He caused our loved ones to suffer because they had done something wrong? Such cruel suggestions only compound our grief tenfold. We will never stand triumphant in our hours of crisis unless we reject such bad theology and shallow religion. God is not a bully in the heavens who carries a big stick. It is not the chief business of suffering people to repent. To demand repentance denies them their right to grieve and burdens them with unjust guilt.

God could prevent suffering if He chose to do so. God is sovereign over creation. God could intervene to cure cancer, prevent accidents, eliminate war, and correct the injustices of life because He is omnipotent. But God has seen fit to withhold His intervention to allow human suffering.

I have heard some say that God wants everybody to be comfortable and free from suffering, but that these things are totally beyond His power to arrange. Suffering, they say, is caused by Fate, or Nature, and God must yield to these greater powers. But if this is true then God is no longer God. He becomes a lesser power to the impersonal god of chance. A God whose hands are tied is not God at all. I believe that God is capable of divine intervention, but for infinitely wise and good reasons, He does not see fit to do so in many cases. He did not intervene to spare Norma's life. He deemed it necessary and better to allow death.

God allows suffering and death, but He is nevertheless good. My wife's death does not lessen my faith in His goodness or His sovereignty. The fact that I cannot see how cancer is compatible with His goodness does not change this truth. My inability to understand testifies to my ignorance, not to God's weakness or badness.

For reasons unknown to me, God has considered it necessary to make us all subject to disease, suffering, accident, and death. Christians are not exempt. Specifically, God has decreed it necessary that my wife be allowed to die without His intervention to prevent it. This suffering, however, was necessary to the completion of God's master plan, which is infinitely good. C. S. Lewis stated this truth: "The tortures occur. If they are unnecessary, then there is no God or a bad one. If there is a good God, then these tortures are necessary."

I find no consolation in the suggestion that God is impotent, powerless before the cruelties of nature or happenstance. Instead I look for comfort in the belief that God has allowed suffering, but that He has a good purpose in it. The purpose may be temporarily hidden from me.

Some would not understand my comfort because they believe it is ridiculous to suggest that a good God would allow His people to be shattered with such agony. They fail to understand that the goodness of God is an ultimate goodness, not a goodness that always pleases the senses of finite man. We are creatures of comfort and think almost entirely of the here and now.

It is very difficult for me to see my life in relation to eternity. I only see the great, deep waters of testing as they wash over me. My soul sinks in depression, the sun sets over an angry sea, and a shadow of darkness creeps across my life. At times I think that life is no longer worth living. I plunge into a forbidding desert, like Elijah, to sob out my complaint to God. Like Job, I ponder the inscrutable ways of God. I shed my tears into a vast reservoir of unutterable sadness. I may blame Him, yet I trust Him and believe that He understands my hurt.

When I covet death itself as blessed relief from the intolerable burden of ten thousand bleeding wounds, I must trust God just as I trusted Him before my pain. I can and I must redeem this trouble for God's glory. In passing through this valley, I make it a place of springs. In my pit of despair, I discover a wellspring of God. I glorify Him with this spiritual toughness in my time of trouble. God's ultimate goodness will be revealed eventually to the wonder and praise of all.

The dimensions of my spiritual stature are not made or revealed in my hours of victory, but in my hours of pain, grief, and defeat. When my life collapses, darkness envelops, circumstances oppose, friends mutiny, family disintegrates, honor vanishes, and reason fails, *then* I can rise triumphant out of the smoldering ashes of life, because of my faith which draws forth God's supernatural grace.

Therefore in this great grief I offer a ringing affirmation that God is in absolute control. I identify with what James Russell Lowell wrote:

> Truth forever on the scaffold,
>   Wrong forever on the throne,
> Yet that scaffold sways the future,
>   And behind the dim unknown,
> Standeth God within the shadow,
>   Keeping watch above His own.

I must let nothing keep me from such abiding confidence. The road is dark and unclear, but God is infinitely wise and good in permitting me to be here. His desire is that this painful journey be one of stubborn, indomitable faith. So it shall be by God's infinite grace.

In the days of my grief, my great turmoil tempts me to charge God foolishly. It is not that He casts me into a black mudhole and leaves me there; He superintends all of the events of my life so that His purposes might be achieved. This superintending grace of God includes events distasteful to me, but essential to His plan.

Therefore I hold God ultimately responsible for my grief because He is sovereign and has permitted cancer to prove fatal. Rather than responding to this truth with bitterness, I worship Him. By faith I trust Him in my pain and believe He is infinitely good in permitting this to happen to me. In time I shall not blame God, but I will understand just how eternally good He is and how this event is perfectly compatible with that goodness.

Why Must I Hurt?

In God's reckoning, to descend is the path to ascent, to suffer is to find freedom from suffering, to taste darkness is to approach eternal light, to become weak is to become strong.

Why Must
I Hurt?

*Why is my pain unending and
my wound grievous and incurable?
Will you be to me like a deceptive
brook, like a spring that fails?*
Jeremiah 15:18

HY MUST I HURT IF GOD IS SO GOOD?
Deep down inside I sometimes resist belief
in the providence of God. I look at events
everywhere in our world and many appear absurd
and senseless. Are all of these sufferings a part of
God's sovereign plan? Or are they merely the result
of chance? In the divine scheme of things are they
truly necessary? Must I believe that my wife's death
and my family's grief have purposes behind them?
Or was the death simply the result of random bad
luck?

Some believe that God set the world on its course
of existence and then lost control over the natural
happenings that followed. According to such teaching, each and every unpleasant circumstance is the
result of blind fate. Things good and bad just happen
for no reason. We are condemned to live under the
tyranny of the god of chance. Strangely, some people
claim to find comfort in such belief.

My deep conviction is that God does have a master plan and that no events are allowed to happen which are inconsistent with His all-encompassing purposes. I believe literally what Christ taught: "Are not two sparrows sold for a penny? Yet not one of them will fall to the ground apart from the will of your Father. . . . So don't be afraid; you are worth more than many sparrows" (Matthew 10:29, 31). If not one sparrow falls except by the will of God, I may rest assured that Norma's death suited the sovereign purposes of God, however difficult for me to understand.

I am not in the place of grief because of mere happenstance. God providentially makes all things work for my ultimate good. Nothing happens in my life that frustrates His purposes. I believe this because I "know that in all things God works for the good of those who love him, who have been called according to his purpose" (Romans 8:28). And "in him we were also chosen, having been predestined according to the plan of him who works out everything in conformity with the purpose of his will" (Ephesians 1:11).

With my finite nature it is easy for me to think I know better than God. I think I should have more of everything that pleases my senses. My flesh does not consider eternal values. The Spirit of God tells me that the truly important issues are immaterial and eternal. In my suffering, the flesh cries: "God is unfair!"

But the true saint believes: "God is wiser than I." When life seems to collapse around us, we think God is unjust or absent or lacks control or is a bad God. But in that formless darkness we must not surrender our spiritual heritage and integrity. We must reject the advice of Job's wife: "Curse God and die" (Job 2:9). Rather, we say: "Shall we accept good from God, and not trouble?" (Job 2:10).

Under the influence of searing pain, medications, and increasing impurities in the bloodstream, Norma believed the very opposite of truth. At times she thought those caring for her were actually trying to harm her. Suffering frequently distorts our perception of reality. If the duress is great enough, everything looks bleak, black, and hopeless.

I may feel no presence of God while enduring great suffering. The extremity of suffering is to cry: "My God, my God, why have you forsaken me?" (Psalm 22:1). Yet this is precisely what God ordains for many of us. C. S. Lewis observed this phenomenon in the ways of God: "Go to Him when your need is desperate, when all other help is vain, and what do you find? A door slammed in your face, and a sound of bolting and double bolting on the inside. . . . Why is He so present a commander in our time of prosperity and so very absent a help in time of trouble?"

God does not calm every storm. God does not usually deliver at the first sign of distress. He is not a celestial cushion against the bitter experiences of life. He does not immediately straighten out every mess, take away every grief, remove every suffering, right every wrong, or insure success in every endeavor. The truth is that sometimes He sees fit to remove from us every vestige of comfort, even the sense of His presence. We often feel like Job: "The arrows of the Almighty are in me, my spirit drinks in their poison; God's terrors are marshaled against me" (Job 6:4). It is comforting to know that God is not against us, but rather, reality is seriously distorted in our minds. That distorted reality is a part of our trial.

No matter what I think at the time, the trials I face are due directly to His love for me. I like what Charles Spurgeon said: "Into the central heat of the fire doth the Lord cast His saints, and mark you this, He casts them there because they are His own beloved and dearly loved people." If I cannot accept this profound truth, I can never stand unvanquished in grief or sing like Paul and Silas in the Philippian prison. If I cannot submit to the superior wisdom of God's ordination, then I can never grasp the purposes of pain, even the privileges of it. God is concerned with making me strong, He's not concerned with making me comfortable.

Joseph was sold as a slave into Egypt, but God loved him. David suffered in the wilderness for years, but God loved him. Elijah fled to the desert juniper tree, but God loved him. Jeremiah was cast into the mire, but God loved him. Paul was shipwrecked, but God loved him. We may think that these are strange ways for God to show His love, but God knows what best promotes His objectives. The darkness of this hour and the loneliness of this grief testify to the symphony of God's love for me. It is a symphony written in a minor key, but beautiful nonetheless.

When my neat little world collapses and events become hideous to my finite senses, I am presented with the opportunity to submit to the higher authority of God. When God's plan becomes the very antithesis to my own will, the toughest lessons of the Spirit become possible. When my loved one lies suffering and dying, I discern how different are God's ways than man's ways. I learn that I must walk by faith, not by sight. I am taught that God's goodness does not always please my mind. The ugliness of separation teaches me how valueless are the material things of this world and how precious are loved ones.

Undoubtedly God has always allowed His people to come under great pressure "that we might not rely on ourselves but on God, who raises the dead" (2 Corinthians 1:9).

One of the distinguishing marks of my humanity is that I want God's power more than His purpose. I covet demonstrations of His power in my life, especially in the time of crisis. I beg God for His miraculous deliverance. I cry for Him to spare me agony and grief. When His wisdom reveals a purpose which threatens or destroys my comfort, then I struggle in anguish against His design.

This struggle Christ modeled for us in

Gethsemane. Since He was perfectly human, He shrank from suffering and prayed: "Take this cup from me" (Luke 22:42). But He immediately recognized that the Father's eternal purposes were infinitely more important than deliverance from suffering, so He prayed submissively: "Yet not my will, but yours be done" (Luke 22:42).

God does not always meet the desperate needs in lives in the way we think He should. Lazarus was not delivered from sickness because it did not suit God's purpose. Paul was not delivered from the thorn in the flesh because God's purpose was best served with the thorn, not without it. I must desire His purpose to be effected in my experience, regardless of the grief. There is no victory in crisis until I learn to pray: "Yet not my will, but yours be done."

So I hurt. God wants to work His purposes in my life. If I need to be humbled, I may fall. If He wants me to be more caring, I may hurt. If I am in danger of pride, I may be given a thorn in the flesh. If He marks me for true godliness, I may lift to my mouth a full cup, bitter to the taste, but healthful to the soul. Each crisis presents me with the opportunity for a stretching, growing, God-honoring act of faith.

I have observed that God sometimes deems it necessary to remove from me the external signs of His blessing in order that the pressure of darkness might prompt me to a new level of trust in Him. In God's reckoning, to descend is the path to ascent, to suffer is to find freedom from suffering, to taste darkness is to approach eternal light, to become weak is to become strong. Each agonizing moment is essential or God would not allow it. To be counted worthy of suffering is to enter an entirely new realm of spiritual experience. My suffering is seen as instrumental, not accidental, to the purposes of a loving God.

I am sometimes more in love with the blessing of God than with the person of God. My peace is interrupted in order to remind me once again that I am not to find my consolation in the trappings of religion, but in God Himself. My comfortable circumstances are shattered that God might be discovered. The blessing is removed that the person of God might be made precious. I find that the greatest of all privileges is a relationship with God, not the enjoyment of His gifts. God will not have me love His gifts more than I love Him.

Many of the Old Testament saints were allowed to frequent the pits of despair, maybe because they so easily measured the love of God by outward, temporal blessings. If a man is persuaded of the favor of God by the evidence of circumstantial blessings, it may be that God will strip him of these things. He is grief-stricken, but he is positioned to know God. In this context Paul could write: "For when I am weak, then I am strong" (2 Corinthians 12:10). To be stripped of personal strength and comfort is to be made a fit receptacle for the grace, power, and person of God.

I am often more concerned about my comfortable circumstances than about my relationship with God. When David went to Ziklag to escape the wilderness trials, he lost touch with the meaning of faith. But when his comfortable world was smashed, he sought God and found a dimension of faith and power not previously known. It is so with me. Trial produces what is better than gold. Peter wrote: "Now for a little while you may have had to suffer grief in all kinds of trials. These have come so that your faith—of greater worth than gold, which perishes even though refined by fire—may be proved genuine and may result in praise, glory and honor when Jesus Christ is revealed" (1 Peter 1:6, 7).

The very fire that blackens my horizons warms my soul. The darkness that oppresses my mind sharpens my vision. The flood that overwhelms my heart quenches my thirst. The thorns that penetrate my flesh strengthen my spirit. The grave that buries my desires deepens my devotion. Man's failure to comprehend this intention of God is one of life's true calamities.

The failure of our modern religion is marked by the failure of many to find God in the darkest depths. To associate Christianity with the heights and never with the depths is to be shallow and superficial. It is an inadequate religion which exults in God on the mountain heights of joy, but does not discern Him in the deep, dark valleys. A religion that only can rejoice in blessings is a poor caricature, a base imitation of biblical faith. The redemption of life's low places is a crucial need of our day.

We pass through perilous days. Let our private affliction drive us to discover the sufficiency of a mighty God. Divested of personal ease, we trust a living, loving God. Agonized beyond power of description, we shout our hallelujahs to His deathless name. Our wounds are open, and sadness is a constant companion, but the heart leaps with the rapture of unconquerable faith in the eternal God.

Can I Rejoice?

Those who equate joviality with spirituality are tragically in error.

Can I Rejoice?

Consider it pure joy, my brothers, whenever you face trials of many kinds.

James 1:2

T HE BIBLE COMMANDS US TO DO SOME difficult things, not the least of which is to rejoice in all circumstances. Paul wrote: "Rejoice in the Lord always. I will say it again: Rejoice!" (Philippians 4:4). Similarly, he wrote to another church: "Be joyful always; . . . give thanks in all circumstances, for this is God's will for you in Christ Jesus" (1 Thessalonians 5:16, 18). James commanded his readers to consider the trials of life "pure joy." At times that appears quite unreasonable, especially in my grief.

Sometimes it is easy to be glad. The soul rises out of the infinite diversity of happenstance into a splendor of exquisite joy. What reveling there is in the delights of God's bounty as they lift, cleanse, and strengthen! There are those glorious moments when I leave the hodgepodge and humdrum for the crowning magnificence of the delectable mountains. Such times are God's providential gifts and I enjoy them to the full. How easy then to breathe joyful praise to a good God!

However, I am learning in these troubled days

that life is seldom a soaring experience. God has called me to walk in the dusty, hot, dark valley. When death rips apart your family, you discover a bitter new reality. I am learning about adversity, loneliness, and the trauma of pain. How does the old command to rejoice look when the sky is so dark, the heart is so heavy, and the grave lies covered with withered flowers? How can I obey the commands to rejoice? Can joy coexist with profound grief?

I know how awful it is when people deny me my grief. It is not wrong to be sad! From time to time someone says to me: "I am praying that the Lord will take away your grief and give you real joy." The unwitting implication is that there can be no joy unless the sadness is first removed. I am not praying that the Lord will take away my grief. Some of the more rapturous saints rebuke expressions of grief with: "What's the matter with you? Don't you know Christians are to be happy? Smile!" Then they quote a text to support their religious exuberance. There are times, like now, that I don't feel like smiling. I cannot let anyone rob me of my right to grieve.

It is popular in our day to identify spirituality with consistent expressions of bubbly, happy emotions, smiling, and radiance. Many people believe that good Christians must be constantly "up" saints. Sometimes we want to be seen as good Christians and so we try to project an image of radiance by hiding our times of unhappiness, negative feelings, and devastating sadness. The Christian life then becomes a masterful deception, a clever charade.

Christianity, however, is not gleeful, uninterrupted bliss. Those who equate joviality with spirituality are tragically in error. Such thinking is contrary to biblical teaching and example.

Few of the great biblical characters were consistently happy as we judge happiness today. Those saints were saddened men, grieved deeply by a world filled with sickness, sin, and death. They were touched with profound sorrow and great loss. They felt keenly the pain and the grief of life in an imperfect world. They wept. David's life, for example, was filled with praise and thanksgiving to God, but it was also filled with anguish, trouble, disappointment, and grief which caused him to weep at times until there was no strength left to weep. Everywhere in Scripture we find those who agonized because they knew the real pathos of human experience. Lydia Maria Child expressed this profound truth: "Whatever is highest and holiest is tinged with melancholy. A prophet is sadder than other men; and He who was greater than all the prophets was a 'Man of Sorrows and acquainted with grief.'"

Consider Paul's words: "sorrowful, yet always rejoicing" (2 Corinthians 6:10). He was simply indicating that in the ugliness of profound grief the Christian is supernaturally enabled to rejoice. The hallelujahs of joy reverberate on broken heart strings. My sorrow touches every part of my life, yet I sorrow not as those who have no hope. My rejoicing is not that of happy feelings; it is triumph in trial and confidence in a supreme God. The true joy of the Lord is divine enablement, not effervescent emotions. The real taste of celestial joy is discovering that I can conquer sorrow through Him that loved me.

Without the weeping, the joy is mere superficiality, shallowness on the fringes of discipleship experience. "The sacrifices of God are a broken spirit; a broken and contrite heart, O God, you will not despise" (Psalm 51:17). Surely one of the purposes of God in allowing my heart to ache is that it might be tuned to the pathos of His own heart.

In grief I walk with the Master of Sorrows, who commands: "But take heart! I have overcome the world" (John 16:33). I cannot know this triumph without knowing testing. The resplendent glory of heaven's music cannot be heard until the song of the world lies muffled in the throat. The trials prove faith genuine. Not to be pressed above natural ability is never to know the sustaining grace of an omnipotent God. Not to know that sustaining grace in dire circumstances is to miss the greatness of His joy. Hence, "Blessed are those who mourn . . ." (Matthew 5:4).

The Emmaus disciples discovered that when walking in company with the King, the heavy heart and the heart burning with love were one and the same. Thus it must be for everyone who claims the name of Christ. The place of grief becomes the sacred place of intimacy with the suffering Servant. It is sacred and joyous not because it is pleasant, but because we are sustained there by the secret consolations of a Master who never forsakes. That is our pure joy.

The place that is awful to my flesh is full of awe to my spirit. To be cast into the deep depressions of life is to be plunged into a hallowed sanctum where my voice is struck dumb, but my spirit cries out in flourishing faith. In that holy temple of distress I discover a new brokenness, a perspective on a transient world, and sensitivity to the heartbeat of God. Tears soak my pillow at night, but my dark pit becomes my magnificent depression. It becomes magnificent because I am sustained, supernaturally enabled by God to rejoice in spite of hurt. I am not pleased with the circumstances, but I sing praises to the living God. Paul and Silas were not pleased with the Philippian prison, but they could sing there.

I find that I do all I can to avoid pain, suffering, and sorrow, but when they come I walk on holy ground. I walk where the saints have walked in triumphant joy. I walk in company with the God of broken vessels.

The tortuous deeps become the fields of victory through a faith that removes mountains, makes distant events near, rides roughshod over obstacles, and joyfully makes acquaintance with hardship. Such faith does not sink in the floods of many waters. We dare not lose that militant, aggressive faith of our fathers. We must dare to defy the damnable forces of darkness, knowing that we shall stand, bloodied perhaps, but victorious because the power of God is made perfect in our weakness. Our joy is our victory.

This road of suffering is private. Each moment is personal, unique, and lonely. No man can feel or share in the pain of another. I cannot really know what my children are going through and they cannot know the depth of my grief. We must tread a private, sacred road alone with our Comforter. The principality of sorrow is the secret place, the anointed place of communion where the sufferer and the God of sufferers do great business together. To discover God's sustaining power in this frightful darkness is sometimes magnificent and joyous. It is to exult in the fields of victory.

I have found a sacred wellspring of inner contentment in the deepest pit. Where hope dies, life springs forth. I feel struck down to the dust, yet exalted to the skies. I am overwhelmed with affliction, but sustained with divine consolations. All is taken away, but I have found riches, measureless and free. The very adversity strips away self-sufficiency and forces me to find resource in the omnipotent God.

When Elijah came to the desert juniper tree, God granted him the angelic touch. When he was confused, alone, defeated, and miserable, God fed him. When he wanted to die, God gave him a fresh revelation of His power, His goodness, and His purpose. The juniper tree became the sacred place, the splendid deep. Elijah's devastating collapse was God's platform upon which He revealed His incomparable grace. God's desire is to do the same for me in this valley of shadows.

I remember that awful day when my family began to be drawn against our will into an ever more forbidding desert. I put on a surgical gown and went into the operating room. Minutes later the surgeon extracted from my wife's right breast a lump of grisly cells. Turning to me, he said: "Dr. Means, I want you to see what cancer looks like." The lump was examined by a pathologist whose voice over the loudspeaker in the operating room confirmed the surgeon's diagnosis. "Dr. C_____, Norma Means has an infiltrating carcinoma." A malignant tumor. The word *cancer* was no longer an ugly word. It was a living, creeping, consuming monster. It shredded our emotional stability. It inflicted incredible pain. It made three kids motherless. It deposited me under my own juniper tree to sob out my complaint: "It is enough, O Lord."

What possible joy could be found in such shattering reality? What possible radiance is hidden there in the impenetrable darkness of death? Certainly not happy emotions. Yet it is the magnificent place of His presence and His choosing. My Lord is here in the infernal gloom. He did not dry tears. He did not still the storm. He did not heal. She who was so precious was taken away. There is much that God did not do that I and my children wanted Him to do! But in the midst of the turbulence there is a quiet assurance. There is an arm that reaches out to encircle and uphold. There is a gentle whisper. There is a Presence, majestic, controlling, commanding.

I cannot now soar with wings like the eagle. But I inch along the dusty road in company with the King. It is a treacherous road, painful to my feet, but He makes my heart burn within me. I find Him to be God of the valleys, and this oppressive circumstance is a magnificent place because of His presence. I count it joy to be here. Here I bear crosses, sing at graves, and discover profound supernatural strength. In this awful sorrow there is communion with God and the true joy of triumphant praise.

Yes, even in great tribulation we can and we must rejoice. We must rejoice not merely because it is commanded, but because faith necessitates it and grace promotes it. The acrid circumstance of tribulation is a daily companion to me, but the God of adversities provokes tearful celebration.

How Shall I Handle Grief?

We want instant relief, but God's purposes are seldom accomplished quickly. Our impatience hinders our adjustment to the burden of grief.

How Shall I Handle Grief?

Woe is me for my hurt! my wound is grievous: but I said, Truly this is a grief, and I must bear it.

Jeremiah 10:19 (KJV)

IN GREAT GRIEF, THE DEEP, INNER SPRINGS of the soul are clogged with very intense feelings, often so jumbled as to be impossible to sort out. There is a sense of overwhelming sadness which leads us to suggest that life is no longer worth living. Happy days fade in the memory like the withered flowers on the grave, and in their place there rises the ugliness of loneliness. How desperately I miss her!

Grief becomes like quicksand, which with a soundless kind of fury clutches at my heart, squeezing from it the very essence of life and vitality. Slowly but inexorably, my mind is absorbed with the awful realization that Norma is gone for all time and nothing will ever again be the same. The family unit as I knew it is irreparably destroyed. The permanency and totality of separation produce an ache beyond description and beyond the imagination of those who have never experienced such loss.

For awhile, in the initial months of my grief, there seemed to be no path out of this maze of lostness and depression. Every passage seemed closed, every light seemed extinguished, and every hope seemed futile. I thought: "How indeed is a Christian to cope with grief?" I knew that I was not to "grieve like the rest of men, who have no hope" (1 Thessalonians 4:13). I knew there must be a way to grieve which leads to satisfactory adjustment to the burden, for I am convinced that grief is not a burden which can be shed like a dirty garment.

It doesn't do any good to analyze grief intellectually as the scholars do. An objective, cool discussion of the meaning or stages of the grief experience is worthless, and possibly even harmful to the grief-stricken. Nothing has been quite so objectionable or distasteful to me in recent months as the feeling that I am being scrutinized by those trying to determine what "stage" of grief is current or what progress I have made toward "wholeness." The feeble, and sometimes ridiculous, attempts to compartmentalize grief and dissect it academically are offensive to me as I live daily with this personal odyssey of pain.

I resent those who try to prescribe or predict my emotional and spiritual journey through this experience. Grief is a unique, personal, and sacred experience. It is sacred and personal because I feel shut in to the consolations of God. Only God knows the inner struggle I experience, and it is natural for me to resent the efforts of others to pry into this arena of fierce testing. God and I are alone here, and great business is taking place.

Few people have much patience with grievers. There is the consummate expectation that no matter how great the loss, the sorrowful should rapidly "get over it" and go on with life as though nothing significant happened. But real grief is something you never get over as you do a case of the chicken pox.

I have heard so often that time heals this hurt. I tend to doubt the truthfulness of such a cliché. Enough time has now elapsed for me to know that grief is never quite healed. Each day presents a new challenge of faith, and no mere passage of time or novel amusements soften the reality of my loss. There are many foul ingredients in the bread of this adversity. Some, indeed, are common to every grief and to all human experience, but others are different. And they are always mixed in proportions which make each grief experience unique and special. It is a bedlam of emotional trauma which cannot be tasted by another.

While the grief is never completely dissipated, the true believer is not left without assistance and comfort. My sorrow is not diminished by trite answers, as though some simple solution, if only discovered, could solve a mysterious riddle and rid me of the pain. I have given up belief in a clever unravelment of the knot of grief. Grief is a problem for which there is no immediate solution, simple or otherwise. My desire is that the anguish would simply disappear, but the events of history cannot be changed. No magic waving of a human or divine wand will assuage this stabbing sense of colossal loss. Since it is pointless to look for the absence of grief, it is better that I search for triumph over grief. I am convinced that such victory over sorrow is both the will of God and within reach of the Christian.

I have found help and wisdom in the experience of a professor of Harvard University. He too had a perplexing problem and finally sought the counsel of the eminent clergyman, Phillips Brooks. He spent an hour with the great preacher and emerged a changed, radiant man. It soon dawned upon him, however, that he had entirely forgotten to ask Mr. Brooks about his problem! Yet, he said, "I did not care; I had found out that what I needed was not the solution of a special problem, but the contagion of a triumphant spirit."

What I needed to find was not that which would make the grief vanish, for such is impossible. But rather I needed to discover that triumphant spirit by which grief is redeemed for God's glory and my own inestimable gain. I know that the solution of the problem of grief is impossible, if by "solution" I mean diminishment. If I seek no such resolution in my distress, but instead wait before God for a triumphant spirit, then the suffocating dust of sorrow becomes pure gold, the tears become healthy medicine, the indescribable sense of loss becomes a wedge which presses me closer to God and conforms me to His Son.

How could I gain the triumphant spirit? First, the triumphant spirit comes to the grief-stricken only through a gentle resignation to what God has ordained. This cannot be a hard, bitter submission, but the yielding of a son to a beloved father whom he knows to be wiser than himself.

I must be willing to lie down quietly on the bed of extraordinary sorrow. There God desires to infuse me with the Spirit that renews inner strength and enables me again to mount up with wings as eagles, run and not be weary, walk and not faint. This is indeed the hour of courage and invincible faith, for it is here a fire is lit that softens, warms, and enlightens a world that is so hard, cold, and dark.

David displayed that necessary attitude when he fled Jerusalem during the rebellion of his son Absalom. To Zadok, the priest, David said: "If I find favor in the LORD's eyes, he will bring me back and let me see . . . his dwelling place again. But if he says, 'I am not pleased with you,' then I am ready; let him do to me whatever seems good to him" (2 Samuel 15:25, 26). Or when David's infant son died, David's response was a beautiful acceptance of that bitter fact: "Now that he is dead, why should I fast? Can I bring him back again? I will go to him, but he will not return to me" (2 Samuel 12:23).

I was taught that the Christian must enter God's kingdom through the gates of various trials, tribulations, griefs, and sufferings. If that is so, let them come, and I shall try, by God's grace, to respond to them with a gentle, submissive spirit.

Gaining a quiet resignation to the incomprehensible plan of God has helped me more than anything. Because of that blessed assurance of God's purpose and goodness, the present loss, terrible in its emotional upheaval, staggers me, but it does not defeat me. In the certainty of God's sovereignty, there is no need of posing "If only" speculations: "If only I had done . . ." or "If only we had tried . . ." or "If only the doctor had prescribed . . ." I leave it all quietly to Him who makes no mistakes and holds each of us under the shelter of His providential care. I affirm what Helmut Thielicke has written: "Nothing will be allowed to touch me which has not passed His scrutiny so that it will serve my best interests."

If we insist on understanding all of God's ways, especially in circumstances like these, we are consigned to disappointment and inevitable frustration. Many books have been written in which authors have attempted to explain things like cancer and holocausts. None of the answers of the wisest of men satisfies our distraught minds.

I remember a bitter, anguished father who seized me by the lapel of my coat and demanded an answer to the question: "Why? Why did my only son have to die?" I didn't know then and I still don't know. It is one of God's mysteries. We can no more search the inexhaustible intricacies and riches of God's plans than a mouse is capable of understanding computer technology. No rationalistic endeavor can encompass the scope or the diversity of God's ways.

Previously I wrote that our hurts are perfectly consistent with the love of God. Sometimes it is necessary for God to remove from the saint the external blessings in order to bring about a deeper appreciation of His own person and purpose. The deeper lessons of faith can often be learned only in the pressure of great distress. However, all of these truths are not offered as a substitute for the acceptance of mystery. Mysteries are matters of faith, not reason. An Episcopal bishop of the nineteenth century, Frederic Dan Huntington, stated this profound truth which I have found helpful in coping with grief: "While reason is puzzling itself about mystery, faith is turning it to daily bread, and feeding on it thankfully in her heart of hearts." All shall be made plain, but only in God's good time. Some things are simply beyond rational explanation.

We are almost always in a hurry, but God never is. We want instant relief, but God's purposes are seldom accomplished quickly. Our impatience hinders our adjustment to the burden of grief.

Some years ago, a young mother came into my study. Her troubles were many and complicated. I had no simple solutions and no clever formulas. I tried to help her the best I could. I urged her to give God time "to will and to act according to his good purpose" (Philippians 2:13). Later that day, however, she took her own life. Those who demand of God instant solutions to complex problems usually condemn themselves to the most bitter disappointment and terrible disillusionments.

Grief, I feel, is best handled by lifting the eyes off of the present dilemma and fixing them upon the great eternal truths revealed in God's word. Just now things are unpleasant, maybe even hideous to the senses, but the present moment will dissolve just as the darkest midnight will yield to the onrushing sunrise. Our troubles are "light and momentary" and they are "achieving for us an eternal glory that far outweighs them all" (2 Corinthians 4:17).

Therefore I "fix [my] eyes not on what is seen, but on what is unseen. For what is seen is temporary, but what is unseen is eternal" (2 Corinthians 4:18). There is no misery like misery occupied with itself. And there is no solace like that which comes to those occupied with His glory that will be revealed in us. "Weeping may remain for a night, but rejoicing comes in the morning" (Psalm 30:5). I must think of the morning, not to evade the present but to make the present a time of victory.

When Asaph was in great distress, horrid questions formed upon his lips. He thought all hope was taken away. He thought that God had forsaken him and had entirely forgotten to be gracious. Then he began to meditate upon the incomparable sweep of God's plan which had unfolded in history. He said: "I will remember the deeds of the LORD; yes, I will remember your miracles of long ago. I will meditate on all your works and consider all your mighty deeds" (Psalm 77:11, 12). When Asaph got his eyes off his grief and onto the Lord's marvelous doings, he then discovered that God performs miracles and His path leads "through the mighty waters" (Psalm 77:19).

Those of us who grieve are in danger of spiritual disorientation caused by emotional overload. At a time like this, perspective is altered, life seems cruel, God appears distant, confusion is rampant. Weeping comes, happiness vanishes, ugliness swallows beauty, minutes are tedious, food is tasteless, and the very meaning of existence is threatened. I feel that "my flesh and my heart may fail" (Psalm 73:26). When my senses deceive me into thinking that all is hopeless, I must respond as did the psalmist: "I have made the Sovereign LORD my refuge" (Psalm 73:28).

Our Lord is constantly asking: "You of little faith, why are you so afraid?" (Matthew 8:26). I must enter the fortress of faith, where I will find myself shut in to the mercies of God. Outside there are the discordant sounds of bedevilment, but here, in the place of refuge, I discover the God of broken vessels who offers hope. I am positioned to offer my tear-stained praise to a living God.

I have descended into the dark valley and my innermost nature has writhed in pain, but in the citadel of stubborn belief I find a living spring and a radiance in the midst of blackness. I worship God who "gives songs in the night" (Job 35:10) and find that "at night his song is with me" (Psalm 42:8).

Here in the depths of sorrow I find there is

confusion: confusion of feelings, purpose, values, direction, desires, most everything. Yet in the labyrinth of befuddlement, there is a spiritual clarity and refreshment that is strange, eerie, exotic, something of a paradox. I believe it can only be attributed to a tenacious grip of faith in the absolute, ultimate goodness of God. Or should it be attributed to the tenacious grip of God upon me? Or can the two be separated? No, they cannot be separated, for it is surely the secure grip of God upon me that gives power to the act of faith, which without sight believes the invisible, the impossible, and the immortal.

There is great music in this chamber of grief. It is something like Tchaikovsky's *1812 Overture*. There is great noise, discordant clashing of cymbals, exploding of cannons, and pandemonium of blusterous decibels! Yet in the midst of it all, there is a melody, haunting and faint at times, but plainly heard through the uproar as the soul waits upon God. Here in the din and discord is spiritual harmony and alignment with the Man of Sorrows, well-acquainted with grief. Horace Greeley said: "Great grief makes sacred those upon whom its hand is laid . . . only sorrow can consecrate."

Grief softens the heart, the fountains of the deep are broken up, the successive moments of unfathomable heaviness humanize and ennoble the deeper recesses of being. Here is Holy Ground and clarity in confusion.

But grief is still with me. Something is always breaking open the wounds, making trust in God not merely an event of the past but the daily, hourly necessity. Despite all of the voluminous roar of my agony and my consequent feelings of turmoil and sadness, I trust and worship God. In that worship, I possess serenity, remarkable and miraculous. I do not sorrow as those who have no hope. I know that "blessed are those who mourn, for they will be comforted"

(Matthew 5:4). Jeremiah said: "Truly this is a grief, and I must bear it" (Jeremiah 10:19 KJV). Bear it I will, and bear it with the fortitude and joy of unvanquished, mastering faith.

Is There Any Comfort?

Many people never experience the true consolation of God because they are looking for the wrong thing.

Is There Any Comfort?

Praise be to . . . the Father of compassion and the God of all comfort, who comforts us in all our troubles.

2 Corinthians 1:3, 4

SEVERAL WEEKS AFTER MY WIFE'S DEATH, I noticed a bumper sticker on a car in front of me. It read: "Happiness Is Being Single." I felt stabbed in the heart. Life has a way of mocking our grief, adding insult to our injury. Where in this callous, cruel world can we find a soothing ointment for the open wounds of the soul? We need to be comforted.

When the ugly chariot of cancer came crashing into our family, our minds were filled with rebellious and sorrowful thoughts. It was difficult to think intelligently and almost impossible to understand what had happened to us. I cried: "What I feared has come upon me; what I dreaded has happened to me. I have no peace, no quietness; I have no rest, but only turmoil" (Job 3:25, 26).

Scripture points to a God of comfort, a Father of compassion. Hearts are supposed to be untroubled and unafraid. Did not Jesus command the disciples on the eve of His crucifixion not to allow their hearts to be troubled? But what is the comfort we are supposed to experience? Comfort doesn't seem to come automatically. How do we find the comfort of God and discover solace for our troubled, fearful hearts? I've arrived at some conclusions.

I must understand the nature of God's comfort. Many people never experience the true consolation of God because they are looking for the wrong thing. God desires that we be comforted, but not necessarily comfortable. Biblical comfort is associated with strength, not ease or peaceful repose. It is strength for the battle, not serenity for the couch. If I look for external serenity rather than internal ability, I most likely will be disappointed. God does not normally make things comfortable for me because His purpose is to make me strong, strengthened "with power through His Spirit in [my] inner being" (Ephesians 3:16). God deems it necessary to allow me to hurt and sorrow at times, in order that the inner being might be made strong and conformed to the image of His Son. However, being made of flesh, I would rather have ease than learn the tougher lessons of the Spirit. That's why I often chafe with the ways of God.

God's comfort does not usually smooth the road we travel, nor does it make us jubilantly happy. But it does make us strong. God's comfort is not good feeling, but worthy deeds. The heart that exults in God's comfort is like that of a champion who confidently runs his course, though with pain. It is not like that ease of one who indulges his appetite. "The joy of the LORD is your strength," not your ease (Nehemiah 8:10).

This means the solace of God's comfort does not reduce my grief so much as it increases my stamina. The consolation is not relief from pressure, but sufficiency for trial. I am not made cheerful; I am made competent. Melancholia may not dissipate for a long, long time, but in the midst of that pervasive, wistful sadness there is the assurance that whatever the circumstance I shall cope triumphantly by the power of an indwelling God. I may be "hard pressed on every side, but not crushed; perplexed, but not in despair; persecuted, but not abandoned; struck down, but not destroyed" (2 Corinthians 4:8, 9). Outwardly I waste away, but inwardly I am being renewed day by day. Such is the comfort of God. Blessed are those of us who experience it in the cruel actualities of life.

I err if I think God's comfort removes grief or unpleasant conditions. The apostle Paul tasted deeply of the comfort of God, but rarely experienced pleasant circumstances. God's purpose is to fortify me spiritually so that I might seize miserable situations as opportunities for the display of divine grace and power. If I think God's comfort is the arrival of tranquility and a happy state of mind, I am sure to be disillusioned with God. Green pastures and still waters are pleasant places of repose, but more often than not, I must walk with God through the stormy deep.

Godly comfort equals divine strength. The comfort is the confidence that I am able, not that I am happily at ease in pleasant surroundings. Hence the true saint can claim: "I have learned to be content whatever the circumstances" (Philippians 4:11). How can he be content regardless of external conditions? Because he can say confidently: "I can do everything through him who gives me strength" (Philippians 4:13). Comfort is the joy found in replacing the "I can't" with "I can!"

I have discovered the comfort of supernatural enablement in the recognition that crisis is primarily a crisis of faith. Every trial for the Christian is a testing of faith. In the exercise of faith, there is triumph in trial. By faith God's people have "conquered kingdoms, administered justice, and gained what was promised" (Hebrews 11:33). Comfort is promised, and it is gained by faith.

When I vented my emotional frustrations to God, I began to gain faith in the midst of the crisis. Spurgeon said: "The salt of tears is healthy medicine." The pouring forth of my deepest agonies freed my paralyzed soul before the Creator. David cried to God: "Record my lament; list my tears on your scroll—are they not in your record?" (Psalm 56:8). When David wept until there were no tears left, he then found a new strength (comfort) in the Lord his God. The tears are carefully noted by God and are therapeutic to man. The comfort begins and the desired faith is nurtured by honestly pouring forth to God our problem. I discovered that as I related to God my loneliness, my regrets, and my great emptiness, I began to trust God more. Someone has said that we must tell God our troubles not so that He might hear them, but so that we might see Him.

In these initial months of my profound grief, it is difficult to think of the niceties of theological jargon. God Himself seems like a doctrinal abstraction, aloof, cold, anonymous. In this monumental pain of my soul, I pour forth to God the bitter wine of the heart. Like the Psalmist, I complain: "You have over-whelmed me with all your waves. . . . I am confined and cannot escape; my eyes are dim with grief. . . . the darkness is my closest friend" (Psalm 88:7, 8, 9, 18). Paradoxically, I find the comfort of God begins by my uttering the depth of my distress to a God who seems absent.

A declaration of distress is itself an act of faith. Perhaps it is the supreme act of faith to feel deprived of God, yet to cry out to Him. Jesus did precisely that on the cross when He felt forsaken of the Father, yet prayed: "Father, into your hands I commit my spirit" (Luke 23:46). Not to feel the reality or presence of God is to discover opportunity for this kind of a stretching act of faith. The cry of distress flung toward God becomes the door of access to the comfort of God's strength.

My journey of faith must move beyond the confes-sion of my enormous need and the depth of my horror. The greatness of God's strength is found in my exer-cise of a defiant faith, a faith that follows the bitter lament with the ringing pronouncement: "I trust in a sovereign God!" Defiant faith sizes up all the formidable obstacles in the valley of the shadow and announces in John Bunyan's words: "I will walk in the strength of the Lord my God." Many a roaring lion is chained and tamed by such stubborn, resolute belief. I have seen that through such faith the precious ointment of strengthening comfort anoints the broken heart.

Defiant faith scorns circumstances, obstacles, and impossibilities. This brand of faith challenges the fiends of hell to hurl their fiery darts, and when diabolical schemes seem to triumph, faith exclaims to God: "My times are in your hands" (Psalm 31:15). It is that tenacious, unyielding trust in God that leads troubled hearts into immortal hopes. One's sorrowful condition becomes the platform upon which the strength, wisdom, and beauty of God is revealed to a darkened world. Therein lies the consolation and power of the Almighty God.

This faith, that I am convinced brings consolation, stamps a defiant "NEVERTHELESS" over everything. This is the faith that Habakkuk expressed in his troubled spiritual journey. His questions were not all answered. His circumstances were not changed. But when God showed His servant something of His purpose and power, then the prophet declared:

> Though the fig tree does not bud and there are no grapes on the vines, though the olive crop fails and the fields produce no food, though there are no sheep in the pen and no cattle in the stalls, yet [nevertheless] . . . I will be joyful in God my Savior. The Sovereign LORD is my strength (Habakkuk 3:17-19).

Thus these heroic saints rose phoenix-like from the ashes of agony. Every cry: "I have become like broken pottery" is followed by "but I trust in you, O LORD" (Psalm 31:14). When God's child is stripped of all sense of well-being and security, he still exults: "Though he slay me, yet will I hope in him" (Job 13:15). Implicit trust in the time of darkness is the indispensable necessity of spiritual discovery. In that indefatigable confidence the saint finds the comfort of divine, supernatural strength.

I still struggle and do not expect to find all the answers to the multitude of questions which perplex my soul. My certainties have been few; my doubts have been many. Yet the bedrock assurance which has held my feet from slipping is the confidence that God loves me and nothing occurs outside of His providential control. "For I am convinced that . . . [nothing] in all creation will be able to separate us from the love of God that is in Christ Jesus our Lord" (Romans 8:38, 39). Nothing can staunch the outflow of God's love for me. Nothing He has allowed to happen is inconsistent with His unflagging love. Bands of steel undergird me in that confidence.

When I trust the love of God in the face of discordant, hostile circumstances, I find my soul elevated and toughened. It is in that toughening that God's comfort comes stealing over me through the pain. God's work is not that of pleasing my senses, but that of refining, pruning, and preparing me for His service. God wants me conformed to the image of His Son who Himself "learned obedience from what he suffered" (Hebrews 5:8).

In hurting, I learn to heal hurts. In hungering, I taste the Living Bread. In deprivation, I appreciate true contentment. In suffering, I acquire obedience. In weeping, I discover the oil of gladness. Through the dying and the ripping asunder of my emotional ties, I dip from the stream of grace available to the weary children of God. Through that defiant faith, the comfort of divine adequacy is made a living, breathing reality. Such faith has been authenticated well by a grand, glorious army of saints who have been overcomers. It is a great, tough shield of protection, the indispensable step to glory.

This defiant faith flung into the teeth of wild circumstances purifies the dross from my heart. It conquers difficulties. It does not tremble before the demons of hell or the tyrants of earth. While yet in the flesh, it realizes the promises and finds God all-sufficient for each tear-stained moment. Finding that sufficiency through daring, defiant faith is indeed the blessed elixir that is comfort to my wounded heart.

My wife and I were in our little grade school orchestra together. She sawed the violin and I squawked the clarinet. We dated in high school and married at the age of twenty. She was taken from me after almost twenty-eight years of intimacy. A lifetime of continuity suffered irreparable devastation. What is the life-saving balm for such a penetrating wound? It is the sufficiency of God discovered in a defiant faith that prompts me to praise God who "always leads us in triumphal procession in Christ" (2 Corinthians 2:14). Therein lies the comfort of sustenance, adequacy, contentment.

Does God Really Care?

In all of this personal odyssey of catastrophic events, there is this rising, absorbing thought: God knows and feels our pain. Just as He did at the grave of Lazarus, He weeps with me. My God weeps.

Does God Really Care?

In all their distress he too was distressed . . . he lifted them up and carried them all the days of old.
Isaiah 63:9

I AM FINDING THAT TO WEEP THE TEARS OF separation is to enter a realm of personal experience quite unlike anything I have previously known. My sheer awareness of loss is a relentless, twisting, driving agony which creates a great void in my life. Emptiness saturates my every waking moment. Wherever I go and whatever I do, there is the stabbing consciousness of Norma's absence. Does God know and understand this atrocity of emotional pain? Is God an objective bystander to the trouble of my soul, or is He somehow very much involved? Does God truly care that I hurt? Does He hurt with me?

Many scenes of sickness stand like unshakeable pillars in the mind. There is a vivid image of a hospital corridor. A year and a half after the first surgery, the cancer had spread to the spine and Norma was having trouble walking because of the pain. One day when I was leaving her room she insisted on walking me part way to the elevator. I kissed her goodbye and she headed back to her room. I turned to see her leaning against the wall for support as she limped in

agony back to her room. I ached for her. In that hor-
rible instant, I realized that I was going to lose her. I
wish that I could erase the hideous memory of that
wretched moment, but I cannot. There are many such
cruel memories, each one carrying its unique, stabbing
pain. Somehow I must live with them. They cannot
be erased from the record of history implanted in the
mind. Does God know and care how great is the suffering of such memory?

At times I'm tempted to believe that God is too
busy for the likes of me. There are billions of us mortals
in the throes of life's ups and downs. Is it conceivable
that God takes note of my individual needs, infirmities, and moments of agony? Is it possible that an
omnipotent God tastes my bitter sorrow, walks my
stony path, feels my piercing pain? Is God an absent
spectator or a present participator in the drama of my
life?

God has made a covenant with us, an eternal
pledge. "Surely I will be with you always, to the very
end of the age" (Matthew 28:20). That promise stands
as a beacon light of hope to God's troubled people.
Whether our journey lies through the delightful
mountain heights or through the billowy deeps of
trial, He is committed to a day-by-day sharing of the
pilgrimage. He is not too busy or too uncaring for me.
My path is His.

I have a tendency to think of God as something
of a giant computer in the sky, objective, cool, dispas-
sionate. I find it easy to think of God as the great
recorder and observer of human history. It is more
difficult to think of God as hurting, happy, sad,
angered, grieving, or caring. Yet throughout Scripture, God is pictured as an involved, emotional being,
not a distant object. My own emotional reality testifies
to my being made in the image of God. I experience
the daily fluctuation of emotions because God made
me in His own image. God experiences emotion, and
therefore so do I. My capacity for grief is a reflection

of the grief of God. My suffering is not a cold, re-moved, objective fact which God notes, but it is a part of God's own on-going personal experience. I could not know the reality of suffering were it not for the fact that God knows suffering. Being made in the image of God means, in part, that I share the likeness of God's emotional nature.

Jesus revealed the emotional nature of God in His indignation at the profanation of the temple. He showed God's capacity for feeling in His tears of com-passion and grief. He knew the pathos of loneliness, the tenderness of caring, the gladness of joy, and the heartbreak of separation. He has borne our sorrows and carried our griefs. He still does bear the emotional disruptions of our daily experiences. God knows expe-rientially the trauma of our emotional riot. He is not too busy, too removed, or too uncaring to feel our pain, carry our infirmities. God has not only suffered for us in Christ, but he has eternally identified Himself with us. What God has done *for* us is crucial, but the comfort in our present dilemma lies in what God cur-rently is doing *with* us.

God spoke to His people in the day of Isaiah: "When you pass through the waters, I will be with you . . ." (Isaiah 43:2). That has always been the intent and purpose of God. He allows us no experience, however painful, that He does not share. It is true that God knew suffering and separation on the cross, but it is equally true that our own hurts are as real and as painful to Him as they are to us now. His empathy is not that of an observer, but that of a sharer. In our meditation on the agony of our Lord when He walked on earth, we truly grasp the profound truth that God has inextricably joined Himself to us in this caring, participating relationship.

I have known the awful experience of watching a loved one suffer and die. I was with my wife as she writhed in pain, both physical and emotional. She finally died when the human body could endure no more distress. I said my goodbyes and heard the lid of the casket snap shut with a note of utter finality. I have wept much, and more tears will come, I'm sure, as again and again I feel deprivation, tragic loss, emotional disintegration. I feel confused, tormented, angered at a loathsome disease. The future is a blob of apprehension because it does not contain her presence. What an astonishing time!

In all of this personal odyssey of catastrophic events, there is this rising, absorbing thought: *God knows and feels our pain.* Just as He did at the grave of Lazarus, He weeps with me. My God weeps.

It is strange and wonderful to think of God as a distressed deity, a weeping King. God enters the arena of misery and the desolation of a stricken family and He groans and weeps with us. This is a mystery profound and fathomless, but I dare not forget it! So deeply is He touched with the feelings of our infirmities that He joins us in the cry of piercing sorrow. I think that the last tear wiped away shall be a tear God brushes from His own eye. Until then, our God weeps with us.

In all of the distress of God's people, "he too was distressed" (Isaiah 63:9). So perfectly does God identify with us that our agony becomes His own, our pain becomes His ongoing experience. We walk through valleys fearing no evil, "for you are with me; your rod and your staff, they comfort me" (Psalm 23:4). The comfort is found in the blessed assurance that He is with us! He is with us, knowing, feeling, caring in all of our distress.

True comforters will mourn with me. The bearers of advice, lectures, and texts are "Job's comforters" and no help at all to me in my moment of crisis. The true friend and comforter is the one who comes with open arms and a sensitive spirit. A true friend grieves with me. Remember what Paul wrote: "Rejoice with those who rejoice; mourn with those who mourn" (Romans 12:15). My God comforts me because He identifies with my humanity and walks the lonely road of grief as my friend. When I am distressed, He is distressed.

Jesus gathered the disciples on the eve of His crucifixion to instruct them concerning His departure and the coming of the Comforter. Within twenty-four hours their world would collapse. They had pledged themselves to a Messiah who would hang bleeding and torn on a cross, then lie cold and silent in the tomb. How would they handle this agony? The sepulchre is sealed. Separation from their Lord is now a reality. Their dreams lie dashed upon the rock Golgotha. They must remember, as we must, the Master's words, "Do not let your hearts be troubled" (John 14:1). We must grasp the promise of the Comforter whose blessed presence is assured for all time.

How is it that the troubled heart can be hushed into the quiet assurance and supreme confidence of the Comforter? A frantic search for the world's thrills is useless. The world's wisdom is of no value to the tortured soul. The true peace of God comes gently into the soul that quietly but defiantly trusts all to the one who said: "Trust in God; trust also in me" (John 14:1). It is in that resolution of trust that the troubled soul, so tossed and torn by tempest, suddenly grows aware of the Presence. It is, of course, the presence of the Master of storms, who rebukes the wind and says to the waves: "Quiet! Be still!" (Mark 4:39). It was that steady, abiding confidence that enabled Paul, when facing the sword, to write: "But the Lord stood at my side and gave me strength. . . . The Lord will rescue me from every evil attack and will bring me safely to his heavenly kingdom" (2 Timothy 4:17, 18).

In my world of pain and passion, calamity and confusion, where this shadow of separation hides from me that which once was mine, and now lies as a mantle soft and silent upon all my present possessions, there is but one way to the serene, majestic calmness of God. It lies in a faith that leads me in all my hours of distress to shelter my soul in the divine comfort of the Master who walks with me, hurts with me, weeps with me.

Life would be intolerable were it not thus shared with God. The hill we climb is so steep, the way is so rough, the journey is so great that the best of us falter and would gladly bid farewell to this world of affliction. Especially is this so when the best of our life is snatched away and ugly memories daily haunt us. But God intrudes Himself into our world of self-pity and sorrow. He brings assurance that the trials shall never be more than we can bear when indeed they are shared with a God who weeps at our side.

Out of the tempest we are urged onward to new tasks, new vitality, and new joys. A life has ended, but new life has already begun, not for any other reason than that there is God. Down the road—who knows how far?—there will be other vicious whirlwinds of trouble, but when they break their fury upon us, they too shall be encountered with courageous faith in an omnipotent God, who weeps with us and who speaks peace to our troubled, fearful hearts.

How Does a Christian Face Death?

It is not a denial of faith to recognize that our personal desires and requests may not be God's plan at all.

How Does a Christian Face Death?

*Only a few years will pass before
I go on the journey of no return. . . .
the grave awaits me.*

Job 16:22; 17:1

NOT LONG AFTER MY WIFE'S DEATH, I attended a funeral service conducted by a practitioner of another religion. His message was that death is not real, but a mere illusion. However, I had recently encountered this hideous event and I knew better. When the grave was closed over the body of my loved one, I knew that few things were more real than death. To stand there in the chill of the cemetery was to face one of the most bitter realities of life. To come home to a house rendered strangely empty was reality made brutal.

Sickness and death do not creep up on us timidly. There is a surprising swiftness and thunderous roar to events climaxing in the graveyard. Life precariously teeters upon the edge of eternity, and the brush of a feather sends it hurtling into the abyss. Man may flourish like a flower of the field, but he will be cut down, sometimes painfully, prematurely, or tragically, in our human judgment. Heroic efforts are made to thwart the last enemy, but as a physician friend observes: "All my patients die."

Since "man is destined to die once, and after that to face judgment" (Hebrews 9:27) and Christians are no exception, how is death to be accomplished? How are we, who embrace Christian beliefs, to face this unavoidable experience? How are we to help our loved ones die? I tried to answer those questions in the dying experience that so viciously pierced and divided our family.

We attempted to recover a distinctively Christian way of handling terminal illness and death. We passionately wanted to make this conspicuous crisis a conspicuous testimony to our faith in a supreme, good God. We desired to say to the world and to the Christian community: "In the midst of incomprehensible mystery and apparent tragedy, we hereby affirm our unshakeable confidence in a living God who is infinitely good and wise."

Throughout my years of pastoral ministry, I have watched many people die. Some die with terrible fright, some with bitter regrets, some with quiet despair, some with agonized cursing. I remember one man who lay by the hour in his bed, slapping his fist into the adjacent wall with obvious, desperate frustration. But my wife died with the beautiful, distinctive simplicity of one going home after a long journey. She quietly resolved to meet the ultimate crisis like a child of the King. My part was to help her die with undying faith, dignity, and grace. We determined that true Christians must meet the Last Enemy with solid determination, simple yet profound faith.

Through the centuries God's people have examined the New Testament concept of death to discover how Christians are to die. How did Jesus die? And Paul? What was their attitude and conviction as the time of death approached? Can we imitate, duplicate their approach to death?

Our common, feverish efforts to camouflage and deny death run counter to the manner in which Jesus faced the cross. As the hour drew near for Him to suffer, Christ steadfastly progressed toward Jerusalem and firmly set His will to meet the appointed time with courage. The sacred record reveals a steady, steely, unflagging determination to accept pain, darkness, and death. He knew of the betrayal, the mockery, the scourging, the thorns, the nails, and the hours of agony. But He never wavered in His commitment to the work that the Father had given Him. In that attitude of firm, quiet resolution, Jesus advanced steadily to meet indescribable, unimaginable suffering and the death of the cross.

We do not know all that Jesus thought and felt as the hour of passion drew near. But we do know that He sweat great drops of blood and prayed for the cup to pass from Him. Apparently there was a natural, human shrinking from the experience of suffering, a foreboding not uncommon to us all in the face of ugliness, pain, and death. There was a dread that needed to be overcome with heroic faith. And of course, He did overcome it.

As the crescendo of agony approached ever nearer, there was no hesitancy in His step as He journeyed toward a rendezvous with Pilate, soldiers, thorns, and cross. He faced death squarely, head-on, confident in the eternal goodness, sovereignty, and plan of the Father. He progressed to the cross with this indomitable conviction: "Therefore my heart is glad and my tongue rejoices; my body also will rest secure, because you will not abandon me to the grave, nor will you let your Holy One see decay" (Psalm 16:9, 10).

Facing death as Christ faced death means that I too will experience natural apprehension, but an apprehension accompanied by an abiding confidence and fortitude. This is that supernatural grace that I saw throughout Norma's illness. Such faith has been evidenced by countless multitudes of Christians in their hours of dying.

Paul demonstrated this readiness for release from the body as the time of his death drew near. He knew, by faith, that to die was gain. He realized that to be absent from the body was to be present with the Lord. When death became imminent, he wrote: "For I am already being poured out like a drink offering, and the time has come for my departure" (2 Timothy 4:6). Death was forsaking this weary land and it was arriving in a safe harbor. "Now we know that if the earthly tent we live in is destroyed, we have a building from God, an eternal house in heaven, not built by human hands" (2 Corinthians 5:1). Here we groan in a decaying body, but we know that we shall be clothed with immortality, "so that what is mortal may be swallowed up by life" (2 Corinthians 5:4).

Hence the saints have met the trauma of death with spiritual strength and grace. The Master's men have been tortured, sawn asunder, stoned, slain with the sword, stretched upon the rack, branded with hot irons, boiled in oil, and refusing deliverance they have persevered confidently until life's last breath. No panic and vexation of spirit, but a gentle waiting for the timing of God and for His upward calling. The world is not worthy of such saints. In *The Pilgrim's Progress*, Mr. Stand-fast expressed the true sentiment of the mature disciple: "The waters, indeed, are to the palate bitter, and to the stomach cold; yet the thought of what I am going to, and of the conduct that waits for me on the other side, doth lie as a glowing coal at my heart."

It was Norma's desire to display that attitude of invincible faith in the experience of her terminal illness and death. I asked her, only a few weeks before death, if she was afraid. She was not. She was not afraid because of the deep certainty that absence from the body meant presence with the Lord. There was beauty and grace evidenced in dying because there was goodness and faith manifested in living.

Someone has said it is not death we fear, but the act of dying. This is particularly true for me after having witnessed great suffering in dying. I confess to considerable anxiety about the manner in which I shall die. Will it be with pain, long and drawn out? Will I have a struggle to breathe as Norma did? Will I lie paralyzed, dependent on others for constant care? The expression "death with dignity" is popular today, but there is little dignity in death. Death is the fundamental indignity. I despise the indignity of dying. Yet all of these things must be faced with the confidence that the testing of each day will be more than matched with a supply of divine grace. It was so with my loved one and I must believe it will be so with me.

How then did we face the bitter experience? We obtained the best medical care possible. We prayed fervently. To be ready to die and willing to die does not mean one wants to die. Norma certainly did not want to die when she did. She very much wanted to stay to see her children come to adulthood and maturity in their Christian faith.

Some people regard the use of physicians and medicine as a denial of faith. I believe that God frequently uses medicine and surgery to accomplish healing. It is not unbelief to ask God for miraculous, divine healing and also to ask Him to use physicians to ease pain and bring healing. If God uses human skill and knowledge, it is no less an answer to prayer.

We committed her to God with prayerful realism. Believing prayer and a realistic evaluation of facts are not incompatible. It is not a denial of faith to recognize that our personal desires and requests may not be God's plan at all. When the Hebrew believers were faced with the threat of the furnace, they said: "If we are thrown into the blazing furnace, the God we serve is able to save us from it, and he will rescue us from your hand, O king. But even if he does not . . ."

(Daniel 3:17, 18). They believed in God's deliverance, yet they recognized the possibility that they might not be spared. It was no denial of faith to prepare for the eventuality of death. Similarly, Paul prayed for deliverance from Caesar's sword but was resigned to accept the will of God, which could and did mean martyrdom.

As Norma's illness grew steadily worse, we faced the possibility of death. That God did not intervene to bring healing is not evidence of our deficiency of faith, as some would have us think. Rather, her death testifies that God is wiser than we are. The plan and purpose of God are not manipulated by our passionate feelings and pleadings. Prayer is asking and submitting, while recognizing the authority of God. True faith is trusting God for whatever outcome best fulfills His purpose, even if that includes suffering and death. It takes a greater faith to trust Him when death comes than it does to believe He will grant our request for deliverance.

I tried to participate in her suffering and in her dying to the extent possible for one to do in another's death. A surgeon told me that perhaps eighty percent of terminally ill patients are abandoned by their families, either emotionally or physically or both. The sick and the dying need one thing more than anything else. They need to know that there are those who care, love, and will stand by faithfully, regardless of the seriousness, hideousness, or duration of the illness. Nothing is more cruel and anti-Christian than to leave a dying person to suffer and die alone. My greatest determination was to ease as much pain as possible and not to leave her to suffer alone.

When she had surgery, I insisted on being with her. I am thankful that I was privileged to be allowed to be with her in that trauma. Through radiation and chemotherapy, I was present. I took care of her in her last months. She and I prayed and cried together. She died here at home, in this room, by my side. On that

Tuesday night I gave her a shot of Dilaudid for her pain, put my arms around her, and prayed with her. Shortly before dawn she lost consciousness here and gained the presence of the Lord. She died with grace and courage, not shut away from those who loved her. She gave us an example of how Christians die.

Undoubtedly we were more blessed with help than most people in terminal illness situations. I wanted her to be cared for as much as possible by those who really did care. Of course, we used hospitals and professionals when necessary. But when the issue came to dying, we wanted her to be surrounded with our most loved friends who also loved us. These devoted servants of Christ were not merely doing a duty, but were ministering the love of Christ to her. A few women, several of whom were nurses, came to the house regularly to help with her care. And how could we ever repay the friendship and love of Dr. Jim Shane, who came to the house three or more times a week to check on her care, write prescriptions, and pray with us?

Our family room became a loving intensive care center, and what she wanted and needed she received without delay. Toward the end she wanted only cold pink grapefruit to eat. I fed her cold grapefruit at three o'clock in the morning. I feel good about all that we did in helping ease her dying. I have no regrets about the care that we gave her. We did all we could to make her comfortable and to help her die with grace. When I come to die, I hope to have such loving care. A part of the sufferings of Christ was that He was denied that ministry of loving hands in the hours of dying.

In doing what we did, we faced the circumstances of death squarely. We believed it was Christian to lean into the pain without denial, evasion, or camouflage. I wanted to taste the sufferings with her. I tried to join in her sufferings and experience the death with her. In a sense I did die with her. In her dying I learned the meaning of "they will become one flesh" (Genesis 2:24). My right, my responsibility, and my desire was to be with her physically, emotionally, and spiritually, however awful, ugly, and difficult. Her death was all of that, but it also was a thing of simple beauty and commanding testimony.

When death comes, trifling loss can become incalculable gain. In these cold waters, when every nerve throbs with agony, when every tissue cramps with spasm, when body and mind lie exhausted, then with life's last breath let me exult in my Lord who stands to receive me into glory. Then, indeed, the glorious struggle is finished. The race is run, weakness is turned to strength, faith becomes sight. The last enemy is trampled in the dust of divine destiny. Let me then, as now, rest my weary soul in Him and give Him back the life I owe so, in the words of George Matheson's hymn *O Love That Wilt Not Let Me Go*, "That in Thine ocean depths its flow may richer, fuller be."

I look at my own mortality with considerable apprehension. I am going to die, perhaps painfully and with prolonged suffering. Through the experience of Norma's death I learned to drink deeply of the grace of God. I saw how awful, how real death is. In the experience of God's daily sustenance, I gained courage to face my own death. My desire is to face death like Christ and Paul and a great host of others, who defied dying with the cry of victory: "Where, O death, is your victory? Where, O death, is your sting?" (1 Corinthians 15:55). For now, I must believe that when the hour comes, God will supply grace for dying. When the hour of dying comes, I expect to walk confidently toward it and not run from it.

Can I
Ever Forget?

*The past must be buried in order to
love the living, seize the privileges,
smell the flowers, enjoy the sunsets,
and redeem the present.*

Can I
Ever Forget?

*But what can I say? He has spoken
to me, and he himself has done this.
I will walk humbly all my years
because of this anguish of my soul.*
Isaiah 38:15, 17

WILL THIS INEXPRESSIBLE SADNESS never leave me? Will my soul always feel anguished? Will I ever experience a day without constant reminders of the gaping void in my life? Sometimes there is the pain of a haunting melody from a love song we shared years ago or the remembrance of a special anniversary or holiday. Even entering our church I often feel depressed, for she who was always there is there no longer. Sometimes a flitting memory is triggered by nothing at all, or by something inconsistent with all rational explanation. There always seems to be something threatening the loss of my emotional and spiritual equilibrium. Can I ever forget?

The memory is a wonderful attribute of the human species. Life would be most difficult without the ability to remember. Yet the memory is a great burden to one agonizing with grief. Dante wrote: "There is no greater grief than to remember days of joy when misery is at hand." Similarly, Tennyson observed:

"Sorrow's crown of sorrow is remembering happier things."

Good memories and bad memories alike bring their sadness and suffering. The good memories are painful because I realize those good days with her are gone, never to be recaptured. The bad memories hurt because they remind me of my loved one's struggle to breathe, and the endless machines, tubes, and other paraphernalia of sickness and death. I have difficulty remembering Norma laugh, so ugly are the memories of suffering and dying. There are also the memories of the times I should have been kinder, more gentle, more understanding. Such memories pierce me through with sorrow.

When death comes to a loved one, there is not much that remains except the memories, photographs (which merely enhance memory), and a few trinkets accumulated together through the years. I would certainly never want to give up the memories, but can the pain of them ever be lessened? Someone has suggested that the secret of happiness is to live in the present so that there will be no regrets in the future. I am thankful that in spite of the ugliness of the dying, I have many good memories. Yet they, too, are painful. I am convinced that we should live so that in the future we have a great reservoir of happy memories.

There is no escape from the heritage of the successive years and the weight of experience which have left their indelible marks upon my soul. I have risen in ecstasy, wept in desolation, tasted sweet victory, agonized in bitter defeat, and all of these moments have left the residue of wispy, worn, haunting memories, hurts, and longings. I have been on the mountain top like Moses, but I have also flung myself beneath the juniper tree like Elijah. I have wept like David until there was no more strength to weep. I have known failure. There have been many mistakes, sins, tears of contrition, desperations, and some times of idyllic joy, peace, and triumph. I wish I could undo the mistakes, retract the sins, revel again in the joys, hold once more my absent loved one, laugh again and cry again in the various vicissitudes as they unfolded in the strange pattern of my life. I cannot.

The past is forever gone, washed into the eternal sea of history. It can never be recaptured except in the dreaded, yet perversely cherished, memories. It is often painful to live with the memory.

I am trying to cope with these waves of sadness. I cannot rid myself of them. The sadness will not go away; it slips into the busiest schedule and colors my waking hours. Tears do not drown sorrow nor does bustle brush aside melancholia. There is that insatiable desire to reminisce, painful as it is. I want to take out some cherished moment of the past, whiff away the accumulated dust the best I can, and play with it, turning it over and over in my mind. When I do, I am stabbed through and through with pain, yet I feel myself lured on to this indulgence of recall.

I have often pondered Paul's statement: "But one thing I do: Forgetting what is behind and straining toward what is ahead . . ." (Philippians 3:13). How is it possible to forget what is behind? Certainly it is not possible in any literal sense, unless one gets amnesia or psychologically represses the unpleasantries. Neither can be what Paul means by forgetting. Paul himself never forgot his past but made continual reference to it. He did not erase the memory. To attempt such would be folly.

Paul in this statement is teaching that at this moment and in all of the coming moments of life, there must be the exertion of all energy in pressing forward toward the goal. In doing this, Paul was determined that nothing in his past would be allowed to destroy or hinder the fullest possible development of the future or the expenditure of maximum effort in the race for the heavenly prize.

Paul remembered putting the saints in prison. He too had memories that brought chagrin, tears, and grief. He had to cope with his past and the bitter floods of memories, good and bad.

In spite of his past, Paul was determined, by the grace of God, to make full proof of his present ministry and opportunities. The past cannot be allowed to intrude and to destroy the possibilities which now present themselves. "Forgetting what is behind" means to resolutely turn from the past, refusing to dwell upon it, so that full attention can be given to what is ahead. Like a runner in a race, we must put the past behind us if we are to run well in the remainder of the race.

A meaningful, fruitful, and joyous life today and tomorrow necessitates a great, momentous act of burial. If I am to handle well the waves of sadness, I must dig a grave in the very depths of my being. Then, with trembling and tears, I must gather together the untidy ends of my great grief and lay all in this sepulchre of the soul.

Here at this symbolic grave, I peer into a misty, mysterious darkness. There is great treasure that I must bury along with great pain. Life itself appears absurd. How extraordinarily difficult it is to turn away from the past! There is so much in the past that I desperately want to hold fast. I am uncertain as to all the consequences of this act of burial, but I know that unless it is done I cannot function effectively in the remaining years of my life. My nature begs me to indulge my tendency to live in the past, for there are good years and happy experiences there. Nevertheless, there must be a momentous surrender of what is forever behind.

This act of burial means that I must continually reject the temptation to think and tell about the past. What is harmful to my present and future is the incessant practice of reliving, in the memory, the experiences which make me sentimental, melancholic, and sometimes morbid. I have a strong temptation in these searing days of grief to ignore the present and to cling to the past.

The mental regurgitating of personal history makes me depressed, immobile, and worthless. I think: "That was a wonderful time" or "Well, I should have done this" or "Those were the good days" or "The events of that time were such and such." I could do that indefinitely, but that process ruins my present, keeps me from redeeming opportunities, and robs me of any joy of life. The past must be buried in order to love the living, seize the privileges, smell the flowers, enjoy the sunsets and redeem the present. Burying the past is an essential part of the healing process.

Reminiscence can easily become pathological, fatal to emotional, physical, and spiritual health. I remember one relative who was plunged into sudden grief upon the death of her husband to whom she had been married only a few years. For three months after his death she relived, event by event, the experiences of their years together, even to the point of retracing a long automobile trip which they had enjoyed together the previous year. She could not recapture her past happiness in her reminiscence. She discovered that the emotional dissonance of grief increased daily. At the end of three months of such self-inflicted torture, she committed suicide. She could not, or would not, forget the past. The act of burial was never accomplished and her grief destroyed her.

To bury the past does not mean that I do not treasure the memory of my wife. She is more precious than ever to me. There is inevitable nostalgia in revisiting old haunts. Tears well up when I look at old photographs. Waves of sadness wash over my soul as my memory is triggered by unavoidable events. But the act of burial means that I will not rummage around in the dusty closets of the past, dredging up details in order to indulge regret, punish mistakes, escape the present, or tickle my fancy with former pleasures. The act of burial prohibits on-going, debilitating reminiscence.

There are many things in my life that I wish I could undo. These things add immeasurably to my grief. I missed opportunities, spoke ill-advised words, committed thoughtless acts, and generally behaved badly on numerous occasions. However, what I must do now is accept the forgiveness of God and forgive myself. Some grief-stricken people feel more guilt than sorrow, more regret than loss. This act of burial ends this torture of the spirit.

Paul remembered with stabbing pain that he had consented to the death of Stephen, but the past misdeeds were forgiven by the grace of God. No longer did he need to agonize and punish himself. Not to accept the grace of God is blasphemous and disastrous to the present and future.

Years ago, a neighbor of mine drove a huge concrete-delivery truck. One day, contrary to company policy, he stopped at his home for lunch. Then hastily he backed the truck out of his driveway and ran over his own two-year old son, killing him instantly. Most of us do not have to cope with such a sense of guilt mixed with our grief. Yet when death comes, most of us are tempted to torture ourselves with nagging questions such as: "Did I do all that I could?" "Why was I so impatient on that occasion?" "Why was I not more appreciative?" When the answers to these questions are uncomfortable to us, our misery is multiplied. Memories of even the most inconsequential trivia can become monumental when they are rehashed and enhanced in the mind. But self-recrimination is not God's intent. The act of burial must include the acceptance of God's forgiveness. And we must forgive ourselves, which sometimes is more difficult.

Self-abuse eats away self-esteem and keeps us from becoming whole persons who experience the joy of the Lord. Not to seize gratefully the present is to despise the grace of God.

Life is a bruising experience. Each of us has our own private list of hurts. We have suffered unkindness, received unjust criticism, agonized with grief. A biblical form of punishment was stoning, and sometimes I have felt like Paul when he regained consciousness under a pile of stones at Lystra. I have felt battered, beaten, half-dead, half-alive. I have felt rejected, fallen, impoverished, and stricken.

It is fatal to emotional and spiritual health to cherish and enshrine our hurts. There is a "poor me" mentality that destroys rational, effective living. Some people love their hurts. The hurts allow them to feel self-pity and talk incessantly about their poor lot in life. Such people treasure their pain, revel in their griefs and bitter experiences. It is easy to talk about the experience of grief to anyone willing to listen. How awful the sickness! How miserable the suffering! How terrible the loneliness! How interminable the agony!

Paul suffered much and occasionally referred to his hurts. Yet he thought of them as "light and momentary" (2 Corinthians 4:17) and "not worth comparing" (Romans 8:18) with the coming blessing. We would do well to imitate such an attitude. To magnify our hurts is spiritual irresponsibility.

The act of burial keeps me from prizing my hurts, wearing them as badges of honor. As I turn from the past, my attention is diverted from my suffering to the magnificence of God's blessings. My monstrous grief contributes evidence to my spiritual sonship and it has been instrumental in my Christian growth.

Can I ever forget? No, of course not. Nor would I want to forget the experiences which have contributed to making me what I am. Yet these memories cannot be allowed to ruin my present. I must make them contribute positively to my life. This is very difficult, perhaps the most difficult part of the adjustment I must make. Daily I must resist the temptation of reminiscence. I must lift my eyes off of my pain and focus them upon the goodness of God, the blessings I have received, and the promises I have believed. The burial of my hurt must continually be redone and the grave resealed. New opportunities for happiness and service are before me. Only by constant, diligent effort to lay hold of them is it possible to turn away from the past and walk without fainting into the future.

What Does the Future Hold?

God's provision has been adequate in the past; it will be adequate in the future.

What Does the Future Hold?

*Why, you do not even know what will
happen tomorrow. What is your life?
You are a mist that appears for a little
while and then vanishes.*

James 4:14

I ALWAYS MINIMIZED CRISIS UNTIL ONE
entered my own home. Millions of people have
been bruised, broken, outraged, and victimized
in our world of war, immorality, crime, poverty, sickness, accident, and death. These harsh realities did
not seem to affect me so much as long as they stayed
away from my door. But when tragedy tapped on my
shoulder, I suddenly realized I had never been im-
mune from trouble. I know now that it could happen
again.

How can I face the uncertainty and go on with
life in the realization that maybe today or tomorrow
there will be a fresh, new calamity? Having witnessed
close-up the hideous ravages of cancer, I must cope
with the fear that the vicious monster will strike
another blow. Three consecutive generations on
Norma's side of the family have died of this disease.
No one can assure me that it won't happen again. Or

maybe some other atrocity will ravage my diminished family. I may well be cast again into the searing blast of the furnace. I must cope with this uncertainty.

Many people, including Christians, do not cope well with crisis. Some choose to end their lives by suicide. Others survive by resorting to drugs, denial, and diversion. Alcohol, sedatives, tranquilizers, and illegal drugs temporarily dull the pain for millions.

I visited a woman who was dying of a malignant tumor in the abdomen, big as a watermelon, making her look eight months pregnant. She steadfastly denied the seriousness of her condition and died telling herself that she was getting well. Denial was her only method of coping. Others cannot clean out their closets, throw away shoes, or rearrange furniture. They simply cannot face the terrible fact and finality of death.

Many people manage the unpleasantries of life by diversion. They escape into a whirlwind of activity or into the lives of melodramatic soap opera characters. They travel or party or work feverishly or play furiously. They never adjust to reality. Confronting facts is just too painful.

There are those who cannot maintain the vigil with their loved ones through terminal illness. They abandon the sick and pay others to do the unpleasant tasks. Responsibility is avoided, the disagreeable is evaded, and crisis becomes occasion for cowardice.

It is to be expected that those not endowed with divine grace and not supported by God's Spirit should cope with crisis by an assortment of masking and avoidance measures. But for us who are servants of the Most High God, there should be evidence of divine power. If there is no divine enablement, how then are we distinct from unbelievers? Of what value is our professed faith if, indeed, it does not fortify us for life's trials?

Our conspicuous crisis presents us with an outstanding opportunity to secure and demonstrate the efficacy of divine strength. Failure to grasp this is to lose the occasion of testimony. It is also to lose the blessing attendant to the stress.

If under duress we simply perform as our godless society would expect, we deny the power of God. Great crisis must call forth great evidence of the reality of our relationship with God. In our trouble, God desires to use us to reprove the world. Ours is an enabling faith. Fortified by a living God, we stand to meet whatever comes in the confidence that as our day is so shall our strength be.

Divine power in crisis is mostly revealed in supernatural courage, the ability to face every situation. Courage is not the absence of fear or anxiety. Courage is bold action in the face of supreme testing. It is inner, spiritual strength sufficient for the hour of trial.

Paul was warned of impending hardship, imprisonment, and possible death as he traveled to Jerusalem. Paul's response to this prophetic disclosure of coming crisis is typically Christian: "However, I consider my life worth nothing to me, if only I may finish the race and complete the task the Lord Jesus has given me—the task of testifying to the gospel of God's grace" (Acts 20:24). That is courage, a holy boldness to face the future, regardless of the difficulties.

This sanctified, stubborn courage is evidenced many times in Scripture and in church history. The threat of evil men was disdained because: "Those who are with us are more than those who are with them" (2 Kings 6:16). The saints faced sickness with the assurance: "The LORD will sustain him on his sickbed and restore him from his bed of illness" (Psalm 41:3). And should there be no dispensation of gracious healing, the Christian responded: "We are confident, I say, and would prefer to be away from the body and at home with the Lord" (2 Corinthians 5:8). Polycarp, Chrysostom, Luther, Wycliffe, Cranmer, Latimer, and a great host of others confronted the inquisition, the rack, the fire, the arena, and persecution beyond our imagination. They faced all with dignity, grace, and courage. It was a courage that defied difficulties and impossibilities.

I do not know what fearful testing lies around the next bend in the road. I would be untruthful if I said I have no apprehension and no anxiety. The fear of the unknown and the possibility of suffering are so common to all of mankind. And sometimes the worst does happen.

While apprehension is normal, worry is forbidden. Jesus said: "Therefore I tell you, do not worry about your life. . . . Who of you by worrying can add a single hour to his life? . . . Therefore do not worry about tomorrow, for tomorrow will worry about itself. Each day has enough trouble of its own" (Matthew 6:25, 27, 34). A judicious fear is perfectly healthy; it prompts us to get physical checkups, avoid accidents, and behave wisely. Worry eats at the soul, promotes distrust in God, and negates Christian testimony. My faith demands that I face the uncertainty of the future in the confidence that in any meeting of affliction, I am held by the tether of God's grace. My way is well known to my Master, and therefore I walk in confidence. No testing will come but what it will be accompanied by sustaining grace. If I failed to believe that, I would be impoverished beyond measure and would deny the truthfulness of Scripture. God's provision has been adequate in the past; it will be adequate in the future. The secret of our courage lies in our confidence.

It is in the manner of action, not in the matter of feeling, wherein the saint rises in triumph over affliction. The wide range of human emotion is perfectly normal in times of crisis. To attempt to squelch natural feelings is false and injurious. The distinctiveness of the Christian does not lie in unnatural emotion, but in supernatural response.

In the hour of crisis, I may be weak in the knees, but I must step forward. I may bow in my private Gethsemane, sweat blood, and cry for deliverance, but then I rise to take up the cross and move toward yonder marked-out hill of suffering. The fight of faith does not allow abandonment, fleeing in terror. The masking and avoidance methodologies of the godless are beneath the dignity of the biblical pattern.

When Paul wrote: "I can do everything through him who gives me strength" (Philippians 4:13), he was not boasting of his cleverness, prowess, or personal aptitude in mastering circumstances. He was expressing deep confidence that in whatever circumstance—sickness or health, abundance or poverty, life or death—Christ would enable him to cope adequately and triumphantly.

I cannot be assured of a painless future. I suspect there will be other times of extreme testing. I can be assured that in those times of darkness I shall live under the authority of a God of providence. He will not allow me to be tried above what I am able to bear.

The measure of my spiritual stature is not determined or revealed in my hours of prosperity, but in my hours of pain, adversity, grief, and defeat. When life collapses, when circumstances devastate, when prospects appear dim, when hope vanishes, and when the emotions give way to despair, *then* the true saint can rise to declare and evidence faith in God. The same God who has allowed the tearing asunder of the fabric of life is the God who repairs and uses broken vessels. So: "Out of the depths I cry to you, O LORD" (Psalm 130:1).

The bitterest drop of adversity contributes meaning to the floodtide of victory. The sinking of my soul in this hour of trouble serves the elevation of my spirit in the hour to come. By faith I can confront tyrants, devils, despair, and death itself for the Master's sake. The bowing of my head as I sob out my grief will lend authority to my cry: "Death has been swallowed up in victory" (1 Corinthians 15:54).

When the powers of darkness gather their forces, I will defy them in the name of Immanuel, God with us. When my heart breaks in pieces, the Great Physician is already mending it. The deeper the valley of the shadow, the higher the coming mountain of light. Shall I not weep with Him who is acquainted with grief that I might rejoice with Him who is crowned with glory and honor?

By the grace of God, I will not submit to the self-pity of the godless. I believe that I must face the adversary in the hour of crisis as a redeemed child of God. I must challenge the representatives of hell on earth to hurl their fiery darts. I must stand as one who walks daily in the confidence of a God of providence.

Travail should form the altar for my sacrifice of praise. Grief must create a pageant of tribute to the Man of Sorrows. Death is my stepping stone into the presence of my living God. The worst of life's experiences must synchronize my heartbeat to that of the Lord of Glory and provide a platform for the display of His grace.

In the midst of my most shattering defeat, I feel the unconquerable hand of the Spirit of victory eternal. I hear the drumbeat of the Master Drummer. I see the triumphal arch and the coming of the King.

I have felt the anguished torture of a collapsing life. I have wiped the feverish brow, dressed the open sores of cancer, and held in my arms the lifeless body of my loved one, my wife. Having done all this with the defiant faith of a soldier of the cross, I testify that the grace of God is sufficient. I turn now to the uncertainty of the future. What new experience will try my faith and trouble my soul? God only knows, but He who knows, ordains and sustains.

Uncertainty and apprehension are perfectly natural. Yet in the future which contains so many question marks, I may step forward with a magnanimous, noble confidence. It is a confidence that God is sovereignly in control and His presence, His grace, and His sustaining strength are guaranteed.

Epilogue

Most of what was written in the preceding pages was penned in the midst of my worst crisis, during my wife's terminal illness and the months following her death. A few years have now passed and I have gained increased perspective. I do not desire to change anything I have written. My earliest impressions have stood the test of time. Sadness erupts again and again, but God has never failed to provide grace. The wounds never completely heal, but the hurt continually drives me to find my sufficiency in God.

When the past is left sufficiently behind, one finds a new awareness of reality. Life appears short and tenuous. Material things mean so little. I see no meaning in life at all except in the triumph of Christ over the grave. It is the power of the resurrection that enables a steady continuance with responsibility and a joy in the midst of sorrow. Paul spoke profound, solemn truth when he wrote: "If only for this life we have hope in Christ, we are to be pitied more than all men" (1 Corinthians 15:19).

Turning from the grave, there is the encounter of a presence, a new radiance, a new confidence for the remaining portion of life's journey. God has seen me through great crisis, and faith has not failed because His grace does not fail. My faith has been toughened, and for that I am grateful and encouraged.

There is in my present perspective a gathering together of a thousand hallelujahs of gratitude. There is thanksgiving for the gracious, beautiful person who was my wife for almost twenty-eight years. I voice praise for what she taught me about life—and death. I thank God for my precious children whom I still have with me. Few things bring me more comfort than seeing the qualities of Norma evidenced in the lives of our children. They are sensitive, caring, and loving in their young adulthood, very much like their mother. I am proud of them. Their constant support has been a blessing and encouragement to me. My youngest daughter has left for college. The other two have recently married and I now have the added blessing of two delightful grandchildren.

God sometimes allows a great void to be created in our lives, but He fills it with Himself and His people. Never before have I known such a continuing sense of the reality and presence of Christ, my Lord. These suffering experiences are certainly not without purpose.

I am profoundly thankful for the assurance I have that Norma is with the Lord, and that is also my eternal destiny. John Greenleaf Whittier expressed my faith well:

> I know not where His islands lift
> Their fronded palms in air;
> I only know I cannot drift
> Beyond His love and care.

I am still learning that the matchless oratorio of God's love contains notes dissonant to my ears, but essential to the completion of God's composition. When I encountered that which was so distasteful to my senses, there was a shaking of the very foundations of my being. Nevertheless, these cataclysmic events and my colossal loss have left their residue of riches.

Reflection upon the trauma of sickness, death, and grief has deepened my conviction that there is an immense need for an aggressive faith for the time of crisis. Whatever hardship is prescribed for our pilgrimage, let God's children respond with: "Nevertheless, I believe God. It shall be even as He has told me." The one who must face life's shattering experiences without faith is surely to be pitied.

Grief has enabled me to understand Paul's heartbeat when he wrote: "I desire to depart and be with Christ, which is better by far" (Philippians 1:23). The time is surely drawing near when the King of Kings and Lord of Lords shall come. Then all tears shall be wiped away and there shall be no more crying and no more death. Without such expectation, we would be most miserable.

Many tears have been shed in putting my struggle down in these pages. Stuart Hamblen beautifully expressed, in his song "Until Then," the ringing confidence I have had in all my troubled days:

My heart can sing when I pause to remember
A heartache here is but a steppingstone
Along a trail that's winding always upward,
This troubled world is not my final home.